SOCIAL MARKETOLOGY

Improve Your Social Media Processes and Get Customers to Stay Forever

RIC DRAGON

New York Chicago San Francisco Lisbon London Madrid Mexico City
Milan New Delhi San Juan Seoul Singapore Sydney Toronto

1 2 3 4 5 6 7 8 9 0   DOC/DOC   1 8 7 6 5 4 3 2

ISBN   978-0-07-179049-9
MHID   0-07-179049-7

e-book ISBN   978-0-07-179050-5
e-book MHID   0-07-179050-0

Interior design by THINK Book Works

Library of Congress Cataloging-in-Publication Data

Dragon, Ric.
    Social marketology : improve your social media processes and get customers to stay forever / by Ric Dragon.
        p. cm.
    ISBN-13: 978-0-07-179049-9 (alk. paper)
    ISBN-10: 0-07-179049-7 (alk. paper)
    1. Internet marketing--Social aspects.   2. Social media.   3. Marketing—
Social aspects.   4. Customer relations.   I. Title.
    HF5415.1265.D73 2012
    658.8'72--dc23

                                                                2012016987

McGraw-Hill books are available at special quantity discounts to use as premiums and sales promotions, or for use in corporate training programs. To contact a representative please e-mail us at bulksales@mcgraw-hill.com.

This book is printed on acid-free paper.

To my son, Joseph Armand Dragon II

CONTENTS

FOREWORD

Your CMO storms into your office (or cube) and demands to know everything you've been doing in "social media," or if you're less fortunate—what you plan to do about it. You take a deep breath and pause, while your mind races at breakneck speed to formulate the appropriate response. Do you pull out your most recent reports showing how many fans your brand's Facebook page has acquired, or do you pull out the latest "conversation audit" filled with word clouds about what your customers are saying about not only your brand but the things they care about that you need to care about?

All too often, scenes like this are becoming more common across companies around the globe—and not only in the marketing department. Much like the digital revolution, which began over a decade ago, "social" has reared its head as a disruptive force, creating new opportunities but also posing risks. In many ways, social media is distinct from its digital cousin. For one, the technologies have evolved dramatically since the first digital revolution. Mobile technologies allow social connections to occur at lightning speed, freeing up individuals from leaning over a cumbersome PC or laptop. Search engines have had to deal with content not only from professional sources but also from everyone with access to the Internet. We are literally all publishers now. On that note—human behavior enabled by technology has evolved. Need proof? Walk around your neighborhood announcing (loudly) everything you are doing. "I'm reading an amazing book right now on the future of marketing!" People would look at you as if you had a few screws loose.

Yet on the Internet . . . no—on the social web, this type of behavior isn't only considered normal but it's expected and has names. We call them status updates, "sharing," tweeting, Facebooking, posts, and so on. If the embodiment of advertising in physical space is Times Square, than the physical embodiment of social media is a crowded market filled with multiple conversations, debates, announcements, deals, transactions, barters, and yes—networking. You see, the Internet connected computers. The social web connects people.

The social web is evolving right now as I write these words. Take for example Facebook's most recent changes and the impact it is about to have on marketing departments across the globe who don't fully realize it yet. Real-time analytics will create a situation where community managers who don't understand how to interpret data will find themselves behind the curve. What Facebook calls "Reach Generator" will now empower page administrators to pay via self-serve and purchase the ability to feature selected posts. This now makes community managers media buyers in addition to content and engagement specialists. Add in direct messaging, and now your marketing team managing your Facebook team also needs to know a thing or two about customer service and issue management. This thing called social media has quite an impact on business, and when it comes to marketing, it will require much more than a talented writer, creative art director, and even a skilled developer. It will require marketologists who are able to study the social web in real time, interpret meaning from it, and integrate strategy and tactics into broader marketing strategies that have digital at the core as opposed to an afterthought.

Ric Dragon fits this description better than most people I know. He's been immersed in the social space blending knowledge of traditional marketing with everything he's learned firsthand from immersing himself headfirst into social media and how it applies to both marketing and business. Marketology will help you understand how social media impacts traditional search engine activities and introduces new twists on old concepts such as leveraging those who have influence (especially the digital kind) and creating a brand's best friend on the social web—the advocate. Ric outlines several easy-to-grasp frameworks and step-by-step methodologies that will help you think and act like a marketologist as you lead your own efforts involving social media for business. The newly connected social, mobile, and data-driven web we now work with and live on will be mastered by those who seamlessly blend art, science, and sociology. This book will act as your guide.

David Armano
EVP of Global Innovation & Integration for Edelman Digitaland author of the Logic + Emotion blog

ACKNOWLEDGMENTS

Acknowledgments are often a section of the book that the majority of people quickly thumb past, unless they know their own name to be included. This is understandable. This gesture of gratitude is nonetheless very important to me as the author of this book, as this book could not have come into being without the help, support, knowledge, collective wisdom, and encouragement of many individuals.

To my family, for their support and patience, and in some cases even some good harsh review with a red pencil.

My partner, Don Tallerman, is the godfather of this book, and Etela Ivkovic, who keeps DragonSearch running smoothly, is the godmother. Danielle Correia gets the credit for being one of the first to help me take a vision of process improvement in social media into a documented methodology. Thanks to everyone at DragonSearch: Claudia D'Arcy, Heather Toboika, Deidre Doom Drewes, Jillian Jackson, Ralph Legnini, Andrew Maguran, Liz Schoen, Andrew Groller, Cassie Allinger, Gregorio Martinez, Clair Smith, Ryan Waterman, John Lavin, Caren Haggerty, and Emily Goetz.

Very special thanks to Josepf Haslam, who not only wielded the red pen for me but also provided some thoughtful conversations about the nature of what we do. Kevin Von Glassitsu gave me some encouragement and direction on some of the deep think around social media, as well as an example of someone who is expert at developing conversations in the social space.

I'm grateful to many of our industry's brightest who were gracious in allowing me to interview and quote them: Stephanie Weingart, Megan Berry, Melissa Richards, Art Zeidman, Britta Schell, Ekaterina Walter, Evan Vogel, Stephen Krcmar, Rob Harles, Kitty Sheehan, Kelly Loubet, Mack Collier, Marcy Massura, Maddie Grant, Stuart Tracte, Robert Hales, Steve Goldner, Todd Wilms, Joe Dager, Zane Aveton, and Rachel Happe.

Of course, as a book about social media, it's only to be expected that many people have connected with me and helped in various forms: Jason Falls, Shahram Khorsand, Cinzia Rolling, J.C. Little, Deep Soni, Denise Barlow, Stephanie Grayson, Mo Krochmal, Scott Stratton, Michele Price, Wendy Clark, and Saul Colt, the whole #USGUYS Twibe, including Brandie McCallum, Liva Judic, Paul Biedermann, Joseph Ruiz, Lee Bogner, Mila Araujo, Beth Granger, and Ben Taylor.

I especially appreciate the many professionals at McGraw-Hill who have patiently helped to bring *Social Marketology* into being: Stephanie Frerich, Julia Baxter, and Ann Pryor.

I'm grateful to many individuals who I've met at social media and search marketing conferences, including Jeff Pulver, Rick Calvert, Deb Ng, Shiv Singh, Scott Monty, Tim Ash, Sandra Niehaus, and Bill Sobel. Liz Strauss has been a special friend as well as a mentor, and has demonstrated an exemplary patience.

My experience writing this book was helped along with the input of many friends, including Dan Schneider, Charlotte Pfahl, John Mallen, Shem Cohen, Margot Carr, Lisa Barone, Rhea Drysdale, Christine Murphy, Jessica Merrell, Alan K'necht, Margie Clayman, Matthew Liberty, Tony Fletcher, Holly George, and Robert Burke Warren.

Having the opportunity to work with many businesses, organizations, and clients provided me with the opportunity to develop and test ideas in the real world. I'm grateful to Jeff Serouya, Larry Ruhl, the Bruderhoff, Robert Nachtman, Jonathan Fishman, and The Grammy Foundation.

Thanks to the New York Society Library for a quiet refuge.

CHAPTER 1

INTRODUCING SOCIAL MARKETOLOGY

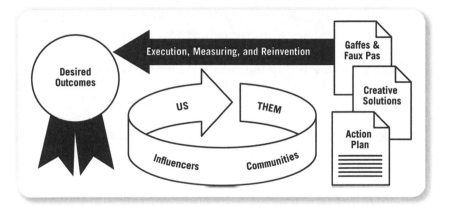

MARKETING AND PSYCHOLOGY

Long before the first business schools started teaching something called marketing, people who called themselves merchandisers, ad men, and promoters well understood that powerful forces were at work beneath the surface of everyday commerce. Even in 1903, Arthur Frederick Sheldon, in *The Science of Successful Salesmanship*, wrote, "We shall unfold certain basic truths of psychology, the study of the human mind. You will learn not alone the mental law of sale, but will be furnished with instruction in psychology, specially written from the standpoint of the business world."

The newly developed approaches of the efficiency movement and scientific management of the early 1900s didn't just aim to improve the productivity of factory laborers but were also used in offices for managers and salespeople. One advertisement in an early magazine extolled the virtues of managers having their very own phone lines as a great time-saver—as a source of efficiency. With time, business schools started offering courses in marketing, thus providing a more measured and scientific approach to bringing goods to consumers.

But in the 1920s, magazine publishers still didn't really understand their audience. They would look around the office and say, "Our readers must be a lot like us." They created advertisements showing idealized mothers welcoming idealized fathers home to their bucolic idealized homes. On another front, highway signage campaigns like those for Burma-Shave were demonstrating that advertising could be entertainment—and that if you could entertain people, they were a little more inclined to like you and purchase your goods. Still, though, it was a scattershot approach to marketing.

In the 1930s, a young business researcher, Arthur C. Nielsen, borrowed capital from some of his old college friends and formed a market research company to study people and their preferences. With the new methodologies and collections of data that Nielsen and others like him provided, organizations embarked on increasingly sophisticated marketing programs based less upon guesswork and more upon a scientific approach.

The 1940s saw greater energy being expended in developing the study of influence: How could so many people be swayed by the charismatic German dictator whose leadership would devastate Europe, or be induced to mass hysteria by a radio program suggesting a Martian invasion? During the war, the military placed a new emphasis on communications and, in the process, trained a whole new generation of public relations experts, helping to foster the growth of a psychological approach to marketing. (Today, a military trained in social media is returning home from war).

Throughout the 1950s and 1960s, marketers adopted increasingly sophisticated approaches to sales and marketing. Different audiences needed to be approached with different messages, and what was sold to those markets needed to truly stand apart and have *unique* value. Those M&Ms melted in your mouth, not in your hands.

In the 1950s, marketing theorist Wroe Alderson (in *Marketing Behavior and Executive Action*) talked about marketing as an "aspect of the interaction among organized behavior systems related to each other in what may be described as an ecological network." While today we might argue that those behavior systems are both organized *and* unorganized, it's telling that marketing has continued to be seen as a fundamentally psychological study.

Since then, we've experienced the heyday of television, which in its own right overwhelmingly became the media of the masses. For decades, marketers were pushing content to consumers, and the only real feedback consumers could give was with their purchases and the relatively few devices that Mr. Nielsen's company had attached to a few thousand radios and televisions.

When Thomas Edison invented his lightbulb, it wasn't merely a lightbulb but an entire system of cables, junction boxes, meters, generators, and switches that required innovation. And so it has also been with personal computing and the Internet. High-speed connectivity, computers with increasingly larger memory, video displays, e-mail, search engines, websites, the mouse, and a lot of other technological breakthroughs that are not even comprehensible to the average nonexpert, all taken together have enabled this vast communications system. We might gloat that Thomas Watson, chairman of IBM, lacked vision when he said in 1943, "I think there is a world market for maybe five computers." And yet, who could have envisioned the complex online system that has become a central fixture in the lives of most people?

Perhaps, in hindsight, it seems obvious that if you were to provide the people of the world with a system in which communication can occur instantly and more easily than ever before, something like social media was bound to emerge—and that along with this whole new kind of media, brands would be in a position to move from shouting from their perches on the corporate mountaintop to actually being among the people. How do brands accomplish this? *They*, our customers, are people—individuals who eat meals, go to sleep, and have jobs or school, hobbies, and lives. How does a brand become more of a person and become a part of the conversation?

It's true that there have been many things analogous to social media before—discussion boards, Internet relay chat, CB radio, and even the telephone. But in social media, we have something utterly different. The many technologies have come together in such a way that we can share ideas instantly and with a specificity of affinities. We can become acquainted with others scattered over the entire globe and forge real relationships in the real world. Out in the world, there is a humongous party taking place, where people are connecting with one another with ease. Brands can join the party too; we just need to prepare a bit more.

Before the pervasive adoption of social media, Web 2.0 was a major topic in business. Web 2.0 is a designation covering a whole range of technologies such as blogs, online chats, and even the film descriptions that pop up within a page on Netflix. As John Chambers, CEO of Cisco, said about Web 2.0, "It's going from 'command and control' to 'enable and facilitate.'" Social media has become the primary tool for creating collaborative environments between organizations and consumers.

FOR MARKETERS, THE WORLD HAS CHANGED

In the late 1990s, the concept of the blog came into being. Jorn Barger created a script that logged the website addresses he visited to a web page (thus a Weblog), and others created software that enabled users to maintain online journals. The critical element was the development of software that allowed people to easily post their own content, and then to enable others to comment. If the politicians who once feared that people who bought ink by the barrel would be here now, they would have to contend with a world where everyone owns an unlimited supply of ink. By the end of 2011, NM Incite, a Nielsen/McKinsey company, tracked over 181 million blogs.

Marketing is often understood to be a black art wherein its practitioners endeavor to persuade bald men to buy hairbrushes. Students of marketing are exposed to concepts like the four Ps (product, price, place, and promotion), differentiators, positioning, and the Ansoff matrix, along with a whole lot of mathematical formulas. Typically, once marketers assume their jobs in corporations, they're expected to do things that increase sales. At its best, marketing acts as that wonderful bridge between those who create goods and services and those who consume them—and it is in that process where true value is created. It is true that in understanding people's psychology, we could use our knowledge to simply increase sales of units for a quarter. This is certainly something that marketing is capable of doing, but the larger and more significant possibility is in creating enduring and sustainable value.

Marketing in the social media is *fundamentally* different from conventional marketing. The depth in which connections can be made with the "audience" or "customers" is far greater than it possibly can be with any other medium. The very nature of influence at this level means that values and vision must be in tune. In writing about how companies are using social media, Mikolaj Jan Piskorski stated, "What the poorly performing companies shared was that they merely imported their digital strategies into social environments by broadcasting commercial messages or seeking customer feedback."

It is my hope that through this new ability to engage customers directly, we're able to create value for those people, helping to make the web a better place, improving our world in the process. There is a beautiful promise in social media that, instead of being hucksters, we are helping to facilitate communities, conversations, and people engaging with one another.

> "We tried to scale it across the company without really understanding what it was we were doing, and so then we had to take a step back, and I think a lot of companies had gone out to conferences and talked to people, they had gone through the same thing, it's the ready, fire, aim approach, you know. Let's go out there, let's start doing something and we'll develop a strategy later, and we fell into that just like everybody else."
>
> —Todd Wilms, SAP

SOCIAL MEDIA MARKETING IS DIFFERENT

As the Internet initially flourished, advertisers rushed to the new opportunities for banners, tiles, and interstitial ads. Online ads could be easily animated to help draw the users' eyes to the call to action, or even used as a tool in *interruptive marketing*, taking over the web page. It was only natural that as consumers spent more and more of their screen time interacting with others in social media, advertisers wanted to be in that space as well. But an interesting thing happened: people went to social media to meet new people or to strengthen the relationships they had with people they already knew. They weren't there to be the target of a company's advertising agenda.

We can suppose a wide range of motivations for people to be on social media—reasons that are based in our brain chemistry, or environmental conditioning, and our basic psychology. In social media, people are chatting about the inane aspects of life—what they had for breakfast or where they're going out for drinks. They are also discussing the weighty topics of the day such as revolutions and cures for cancer. The interesting thing is that the gossipy chitchat may have a critical role in the larger thinking.

British psychologist Robin Dunbar has suggested that social grooming, or allo-grooming, is a basic behavior in mammals in general and even more so in primates. In picking nits and smoothing their companions' hair, our animal cousins are creating bonds that help to establish who should come to another's aid in a crisis. In humans, social grooming has extended itself into language as chitchat. When people on Twitter say, "please pass the #coffee" or other such small talk, they're establishing a baseline of safety for a deeper, more meaningful conversation. Studies have also shown that in social grooming we experience increased levels of dopamine, oxytocin, and endorphins. Dopamine is the neurotransmitter that provides us with a little surge of enthusiasm. It's one of the brain's most powerful reward systems.

In the study of addictive behavior, it has been determined that small and unexpected payoffs are an important motivator. You don't need to win the jackpot every time for gambling to be addictive—you just need to win every so often and, most important, unexpectedly. That stimulus from gambling stimulates the brain's production of dopamine. Social media is rife with little unexpected payoffs. Every time someone "likes" something you write, follows you, becomes your friend, or retweets or "pluses" you, you are receiving a small payoff. So, in social media, there are multiple types of transactions, each contributing in its own way to our sense of well-being.

Of course, it would be a wild oversimplification to think of social media as a big addictive system, giving people small injections of neurotransmitters that make them feel good. Nor do I advocate any idea that marketers should exploit people's vulnerabilities. People are enjoying themselves. Social media is entertainment, too. People are social creatures. It's important for marketers to understand all of the elements that help to make social media so viral, engaging, and popular.

SOCIAL ORGANIZATION

A powerful concept that has been gaining momentum is that of an organization becoming a *social organization*, from top to bottom. In some types of organizations, and at a certain scale, it makes sense for an entire organization to be social—for people throughout the organization to become involved with all types of media. Social media can be a listening and response post for customer feedback; it can be used to harvest new ideas for product development; and it can help to discover where existing products aren't quite making the grade. The organization's leadership can be actively involved in talking with customers. Smart organizations *will* ultimately integrate social media throughout the organization. In some instances, customer care might take the lead, or public relations and communications might, or even product development; but in many circumstances, marketing will take the leadership role and provide training and governance. And in doing so, marketing can take on the role that is often imagined for it, where it isn't just about supporting sales but is about truly helping the organization create value in connecting with consumers.

For some organizations, the challenges to fulfilling a vision of organizationwide social media will be too great. (The risk of not becoming a social organization is that once a competitor does, that company is going to take a lot of ground that will be difficult to recover.) There is also a difference between brand-centric social media and organization-centric social media; the choice of direction will depend on the makeup of your organization. As David Armano of Edelman has written, "A social brand is what your customer feels (perhaps being engaged on social platforms as part of the customer experience), while a social enterprise internalizes social as part of the way employees collaborate and how the business interacts with partners. The two, add up to doing business in a social and connected way."[1]

THE BASICS

There are three basic activities that must be executed in social media no matter what—even before fulfilling an action plan:

- ▶ Claiming real estate
- ▶ Creating policy
- ▶ Monitoring

Whatever your commitment to social media, you'll want to claim your profiles in every credible social media platform. We call that "owning the real estate." You wouldn't want your competition getting its name on Facebook before you—or, for that matter, on any other platform, since we really have no way of knowing which ones will take off. Another positive here is the potential value to your own website's search engine optimization (backlink value). Often, on social media profiles, you're able to include a brief bio, description, and even keywords. Make these relevant to what you do so that the cloud of keywords around the link back to your site is relevant.

THREE PREMISES

Many books have been written on the topic of social media in general and how it fits into marketing in particular. Most of those books fall into one of two categories: the evangelical and the tactical. The evangelical books are necessary—much of the change in business that is coming about as a result of social is on the verge of being revolutionary. There can be a lot of reluctance on the part of executives to embrace this change, as it requires a different mindset than the pre–social media paradigm. The tactical books are important, too, as many businesses, particularly small businesses, need guidance in the actual implementation of each of the social channels. However, this book is neither: I aim to address the elements that are crucial to the development of a larger social media strategy and the steps for implementing this strategy.

This book is based on three premises: The first is that social media behaviors follow patterns. By understanding these patterns, we can work within an area that is otherwise a seeming maelstrom of new information and change. The second premise is that not only is it viable for social media marketing to be brought within a process, but real value can be added to an organization that does so. The third premise is that not all social media projects are the same. We tend to lump it all under that one big heading of "social media," whereas in reality there are many different types of projects.

THE PROCESS

The social media marketing process I'm introducing here includes a fundamental framework that will provide the foundation for any type of project. It is based on these basic steps:

1. Focusing on desired outcomes: vision, goals, and objectives metrics
2. Incorporating knowledge and development of the brand personality and voice
3. Identifying the smallest segments possible of your audiences, customers, users, or constituents
4. Identifying the communities that those microsegments belong to—how people behave in those communities and what they are saying
5. Identifying the influencers of those communities
6. Creating an action plan for your project
7. Execution, measuring, and reinvention of social media activities and programs

The steps following desired outcomes, through to the action plan, may be entered at different places, depending on the nature of your organization. For instance, you may have a strong sense of the community in which you belong and prefer to create your voice based on that community. (MTV is a good example of an organization that does this.) Or, conversely, you may wish to work from voice, to microaudiences, to communities, to influencers.

This book also deals with two important tangents: creative campaigns and reputation management. Interspersed throughout this book, within the discussion of each major process step, I'll also be addressing the different types of marketing projects that relate to the step.

There are seven main different types of social media projects that will be covered in this book. These are the big-picture type of endeavors, which means that any particular organization's efforts can comprise a combination of these activities.

- ▶ **Brand beachhead.** This is the social media project wherein the brand equity is maintained, making sure that we've created profiles in the social media platforms that are relevant, that we're monitoring, and that we're being responsive to.
- ▶ **Influencer outreach project.** Here, we identify and focus on the more influential people within a topic area, with the objective of getting them to recognize our brand and to engage with it in a meaningful capacity.
- ▶ **Community-building social media project.** Whether we join an existing community or create a new one, this is the project wherein we aim to build a more robust community, where if ours is not a major voice, at least it's part of the conversation.
- ▶ **The big splash project.** This is the social media project that tends to get written about in the press, such as the Old Spice campaign or the Night Agency's new Doritos Uncut campaign. The hallmark here is creativity.
- ▶ **Employee brand ambassador project.** This is building up a group of individuals inside the organization who will become a part of the brand's social outreach. Support services, training, and guidance can help create an army of social media users who will extend the reach of marketing and communications beyond the limits of the marketing and PR teams.
- ▶ **Customer brand ambassador program project.** The customer-based brand ambassador program empowers a set of people outside the company to advocate for the brand. Ideally, it's not a relationship that's based on you giving these customers money, but instead it's one where you give them access to leadership and information and help amplify the passion they feel for your brand.
- ▶ **The crisis project.** Whether before a crisis occurs or after, this project aims to mitigate damage through social media.

This book is not meant to be definitive. As has been heard at many a social media conference, none of us are experts but all of us are students. Social media has been developing quickly, so quickly, in fact, that the industry is going to be identifying and developing best practices for a long time to come. New social media platforms are going to be developed that might present new ways of interacting or require new policies. We need a framework for understanding the underlying patterns and for working within this changing environment.

Because of this constant change, it isn't within the purview of this book to address particular social platforms or particular tactics. Marketing leaders need a framework in which to work with any new social media platform, or with tactics that might emerge from those platforms. In creating strategies, we need to be able to define our approach within a framework that we can communicate both upward and downward in the organization so that stakeholders throughout the enterprise can buy in to the strategy and help to make it a reality.

Social media exists within a larger marketing and communications ecosystem that is, at the topmost level, driven by organizational culture, values, mission, and vision. These organizational attributes then define the brand, which in turn provides a value proposition to customers. The overall marketing and communications ecosystem includes all of the points where the customer or people influencing the customer are touched by the brand. In the traditional landscape, this included PR, print, television, radio, events, and direct mail. Today, it also includes digital channels: organic and paid search via Google, Bing, and other search engines as well as online display and mobile (Figure 1.1). The third dimension is social, which supports and is supported by both traditional and digital communications.

Further complicating the role of marketing and social media is that social media can be a part of the fabric of an entire organization's communications, not just marketing. Customer service, human resources, leadership, product development, and every other component of the organization can become part of an open system of communication, creating organizations that are richer and more connected with customers. There is a lot of argument over who should "own" social media in organizations, and in fact, this book is dedicated to how it relates to marketing. That doesn't mean it should stop there.

Social media needs are going to vary from organization to organization or from brand to brand. How teams are set up, or

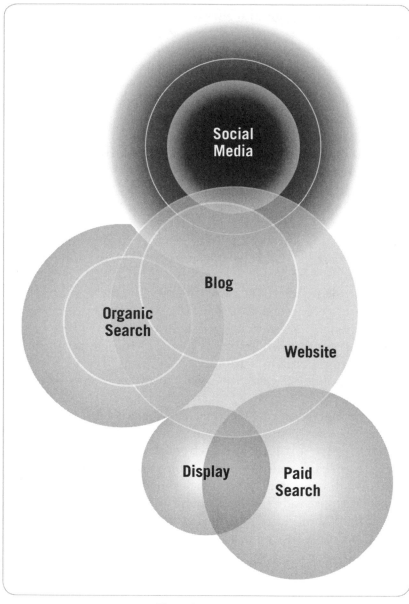

FIGURE 1.1 The online marketing landscape

even how work is executed, will need to vary. Some companies will need very strict procedures in place to vet all outgoing messages, while others will be able to play on the edge of extreme agility. Thus, one of the challenges of this book is that so much is couched in the terms "probably" or "in most cases." Each social media leader will need to find his or her own way with many of these elements. What should be universal is the path through desired outcomes, brand voice, hypersegmentation, communities, and influencers.

It's been suggested that there are some endeavors in this world that are too complex to quantify or to control with processes—and that social media in marketing might be one of them. This book endeavors to counter that claim with approaches, best practices, and processes to work within the complexity of social exchange so that businesses won't get bogged down in bureaucratic response systems and can respond with even greater agility and velocity.

● ● ●

For additional resources, please visit http://www.dragonsearch marketing.com/social-marketology/.

CHAPTER 2

DÉJÀ VU
PATTERNS IN SOCIAL MEDIA

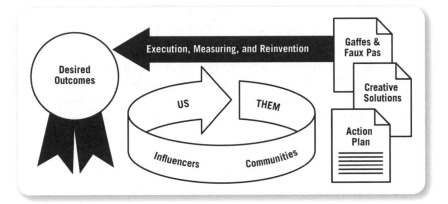

INTRODUCTION TO PATTERNS

It was a late afternoon during the summer break of 1969—a month before the historic Woodstock Festival, for which I was altogether too young. But I do remember watching the television broadcast of Neil Armstrong taking that first step onto the moon's surface and being told to *pay attention*, that *history is being made*. Some events are so special that you have no doubt you are, indeed, witnessing the stuff of legend. At other times, radical changes around us can be so confusing that we often miss the fact that we have seen them before—that while the booted foot belongs to a different person and the surface is another planet, people have been exploring new places since time immemorial.

Social media isn't simply another marketing channel; rather, it constitutes fundamental shifts in how the ecological network of marketing functions—changes different enough to set any marketer's head spinning. Not only are there countless platforms, but new social media sites are being introduced weekly. Existing platforms are undergoing changes, too, as consumers adapt and modify behaviors with new technologies.

People behave differently on various social media platforms, and sometimes different communities using the same social platforms behave in divergent ways. For instance, both marketing professionals and people interested in celebrities have been drawn to Twitter. According to one study, there is a greater interest in celebrity and entertainment in the African American demographic, where urban youth have been using the 140 character limitation for a new style of urban humor.[1]

Middle-aged women have flocked to Farmville, the popular Facebook game, while Millennials use both Facebook and mobile texting. It's not that the lines are clearly demarcated—there is certainly a blurring of usage—but some clear trends have emerged.

In order to tease out the components of specific social platforms and of social media technology in general, it helps to back up and see the underlying patterns. In *A Pattern Language*, a 1977 book on architecture, building, and community planning, the authors write about the language they developed for understanding physical architecture and communities: "The elements of this language are entities called patterns. Each pattern describes a problem which occurs over and over again in our environment, and then describes the core of the solution to that problem, in such a way that you can use this solution a million times over, without ever doing it the same way twice." In this landmark book, which has become a classic in architecture, the authors describe 253 such patterns. People have occupied buildings and villages for millennia; in social media, we're only just beginning to see the underlying patterns, and, doubtless, many more are yet to be invented and identified.

Behavioral patterns and interface patterns exist throughout the web. The term *pattern* is typically used to describe a small piece of repeated functionality in web and application development. For instance, on log-in pages, the "I forgot my password" functionality is ubiquitous—it's a pattern. A contact form with a "thank-you" message on the following page is also a pattern. When the Internet was young, many patterns often competed to fulfill the same purpose, with an ensuing Darwinian winnowing revealing the winners. While many patterns have become accepted as norms, others have faded into obscurity. When customers use e-commerce sites, they have come to expect an "add to cart" and a "checkout," and that after submitting their shipping and billing info, they will be redirected to an order acknowledgment page. The norms we've come to expect are those very patterns.

It's been suggested that social media has really always been around. After all, to be social simply means to be in companionship with another person. Thus, as this line of thinking goes, sitting around the campfire and telling stories is social media. And if you want to be a bit more purist about it, then certainly the telephone (particularly during the days of party lines) would have qualified as social media, along with ham and CB radio.

This new phenomenon that we call social media, though, is fundamentally different. Built on computer-based communications, social media inherently possesses elements of growth. Growth is built into its DNA. The learning curve is extremely short. Most people are able to use social media with ease, enabling them to reach out and connect with people more readily than at any time in history since the days of smaller, stable communities.

On the CB radio, I could meet and speak with dozens of new people in a day. On Internet-based social media, not only does the volume of people I can connect with increase, but because of the nature of computing, I'm able to connect on the very fringes of my thinking and interests.

As the Internet developed in concurrence with the personal computer, the computer became much more than a device for bookkeepers and data managers. Paired with squawky modems that connected over telephone lines, the computer quickly emerged as a means for people living hundreds or even thousands of miles apart to share their particular interests with like-minded strangers. A proliferation of bulletin boards, Internet Relay Chats (IRCs), and Multi-User Dungeons (MUDs) ensued. The idea of a computer simply being an appliance to assist humans with spreadsheets and word processing was quickly obviated; the personal computer had become an entirely new communications platform.

If there were a website where all you could do was post your latest thoughts—and *no one could respond*—that would hardly be social media. The Internet becomes social media once people can respond to one another. That ability is the very essence of social media as we mean it in the world of computer communications. Some people have even suggested that social media goes beyond the duality of two people communicating and requires the possibility that a third might be listening![2] The inherent virtue of contemporary social media is that, thanks to the law of exponential growth, you can communicate with and influence hundreds or even thousands of other people. Exponential growth is the same universal law in effect that prevents you from folding any piece of paper in half more than 12 times, or that allows you to connect with anyone in the world through six connections. It means that, at least in the abstract, if your connections grow exponentially, you can connect with and influence large numbers of relevant people and they, in turn, are able to communicate and influence you.

Various patterns of social media are still being devised. With the sheer volume of people participating, creators of social media platforms are able to incorporate user feedback and introduce innovations and revisions quickly, resulting in a rapidly changing medium. And with each new platform, we benefit by identifying the old patterns as well as the new. Many of the newest innovations in social media aren't coming from mainstream platforms like Facebook, Twitter, and Google Plus but from other sites that are being used daily by millions of people—sites like OkCupid, a dating site, or ASmallWorld, a gated community social media site that requires an invitation from another member. Systems are even being developed that modify themselves to fit user behavior. Like the college campus developers who postpone installing sidewalks until they see the "desire lines," or paths made by people in the grass, these new systems become smarter as people use them.

In the visual arts, fledgling artists are taught to see patterns and structures. If you view a painting or landscape through a piece of orange translucent plastic, the plastic will filter out the blues and you will see certain patterns created by the filtered light. Repeat the process with other colors and other patterns will emerge. Completely desaturate an image of all color, and you will see still more heretofore invisible structures. When you spend your time looking for patterns, it becomes second nature. Writers, actors, poets, sculptors, and other artists also acquire this facility in their respective fields.

Social media could be said to present "wicked problems," which are complex because of their constant change, contradictory information points, and invisible influences. With understanding of the underlying structure of social media, cogent forms start to emerge. Marketers begin to have an environment in which most of their efforts can be worked into processes and in which room can be made for creative solutions that provide sustained value.

In literature studies, it's said that there are only 10 or so stories in the world—that all novels, plays, and movies somehow fit these archetypes. The same is true for social media sites.

Patterns of social communications can be said to fall into two categories: patterns of engagement and patterns in social media platforms.

PATTERNS OF ENGAGEMENT

With origins in the concept of pledging, the word *engagement* possesses strong connotations in war and marriage. If I kneel on bended knee and ask for the hand of my beloved in holy matrimony and she responds in the affirmative, then we have pledged ourselves to be married and are thereby engaged. In another time, knights of yore pledged their allegiance to a king or queen and, in doing so, stood ready to engage in battle.

Today, to "engage the enemy" usually means that you exchange gunfire. In the context of marketing, an advertising firm would have an engagement with its client. Comedians and musicians get club engagements, and consultants get long-term engagements. To engage means to become entangled with, even to attract and hold attention. But the idea of organizations using engagement with customers as a major component of marketing is relatively new.

In 2006, Joe Plummer, the chief research officer at the Advertising Research Foundation (ARF) presented the foundation's working definition of *engagement*: "Engagement is turning on a prospect to a brand idea enhanced by the surrounding context." In 2007, Forrester Research called engagement marketing's new key metric, defining it as "the level of involvement, interaction, intimacy, and influence an individual has with a brand over time."

Engaging with the customer involves an exchange of words and thoughts. If a customer drives down the highway and sees one of our billboards, or if he sees one of our Super Bowl spots, it's true, we could say he has engaged with us, albeit only in the weakest of ways. No person representing the brand is present when the consumer takes in such messages. So if Joe looks at the billboard and says, "What a crock, that sure is an ugly billboard," we don't hear him. The same is true if Jane, while watching that Super Bowl spot, says, "Cool, I'd love to know more about your potato chips." The feedback doesn't reach us. To call that *engagement* is really a stretch.

In an ideal world, we'd be able to have a conversation with customers anytime they're exposed to our brands. Before getting down to business, we might do the things people do, share a snack and chat a bit about life. But of course this is only fantasy. One-on-one engagements simply aren't scalable. We have to use the media that's available to get our messages out. Social media, however, can move us closer to the ideal.

On the social media game site Empire Avenue, users can create small advertisements urging others to buy their stock. In one such ad, mobile application developer Casey Choma lampooned those ads with his own:

> (Witty Comment) (Self Promotion) (Financial Strategy)
> (Inspirational Thought) (Subliminal Message) (Emotional
> Connection) (Reward)

What Casey did was to recognize the general pattern of the ads. Likewise, much of the communication in social media follows patterns. Twitter is a particularly good medium to study patterns, primarily because of the brevity of tweets. In Google Plus and Facebook, communications can be more extensive, and thus a bit more difficult to categorize.

On Twitter, tweets generally fit into these categories:

- ▶ Retweets
- ▶ Sharing of news, inspiration, or entertainment
- ▶ Broadcasting
- ▶ Dialogue (replies to someone in conversation)
- ▶ Expressions of gratitude
- ▶ Social chatter
- ▶ Requests for help and replies

Each of these categories can be further broken down as needed. Community broadcasts, for example, often fall into subcategories such as self-promotion or the advocacy of humanitarian causes.

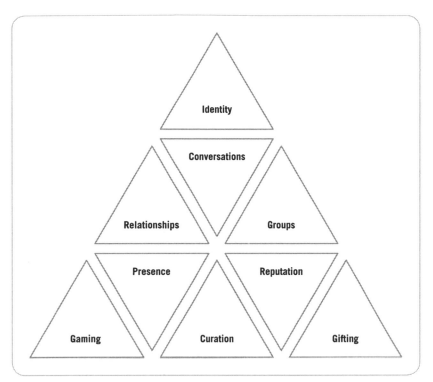

FIGURE 2.1 Social pyramid diagram, indicating the major elements of social media platforms

PATTERNS IN SOCIAL MEDIA PLATFORMS

Any social media platform can be viewed as a collection of tools that allows users to (1) establish relationships, (2) possess attributes, and (3) perform activities in the online world. Within these three major areas are nine significant devices (Figure 2.1):

1. **Identity**—a means of allowing individuals to identify themselves and see the identities of others. On most platforms, these are *profiles*.
2. **Relationships**—a way for people to establish a relationship, such as friends, family, and coworkers.
3. **Conversations**—a means for people within the system to communicate back and forth.
4. **Groups**—a means for people to aggregate into affinity groups.

5. **Gaming**—a means for people to engage in games with each other or the system.
6. **Presence**—a means for people to know who is present or for people to allow their presence to be known, either online or physically.
7. **Curation**—the ability for people to share content.
8. **Reputation**—devices for the establishment of status.
9. **Gifting**—a means for people to give to one another, either very small tokens of status or recognition.

"Boyd's [work] followed the logic that since we cannot predict exactly what a future war might look like, we need to find general patterns, the 'common elements' as he termed them, that will apply to any battle, conflict, or war."

—**Chet Richards** on John Boyd in *Certain to Win*

Identity

If Alexander Graham Bell had had his way, we would all be answering the telephone with a resolute, "Ahoy!" Instead, Bell's arch-rival, Thomas Edison, prevailed with his "hello."[3] It seems every form of electronic communication begins with an opening greeting, including some declaration of who you are.

Absolute anonymity is rare in social media. In some form or another, users define themselves. We might look at this as self-branding, displaying one's shingle, or putting on a mask. The behavior could also be likened to warriors of old exhibiting particular scar patterns to communicate their conquests, or hanging their coats of arms over their doors. For all, creating a profile tells other members of the community who you are. You are identifying yourself.

A profile also acts as a filter, helping to attract the right types of relationships so you can form the right affinity groups for yourself.

The act of self-identification also signals others with whom you wish to form relationships that you're approachable. There would be no purpose in declaring yourself and then refusing all relationships. By creating a profile, you are essentially saying, "I'm open for business."

User profiles are fairly ubiquitous in social media. The salient difference among top social media platforms lies in how much users can customize the look and feel of their profile pages. On some platforms, little to nothing can be done, while on others, such as YouTube and Twitter, users enjoy a lot of latitude in self-expression.

Not all social media sites allow brands or organizations to have an identity. On Facebook, brands can have pages, but they can't invite people to join the page. On LinkedIn, companies are entities that individuals belong to. On Twitter, however, a brand acts in the same capacity as an individual.

Relationships

Almost all social media websites have a function in which users create connections with other users. Open forums or discussion boards are an interesting exception, as they are basically open groups; the relationship is formed simply by virtue of being allowed onto the forum.

Sometimes relationships have reciprocity, sometimes not. I can follow President Barack Obama on Twitter, but it's unlikely he'll follow me back. "Friends" on Facebook are tacitly reciprocal, although one person's privacy settings can make the relationship extremely uneven. On LinkedIn, you have to invite an individual into your network. In smaller social networks, there aren't features enabling a special relationship between two people; the smallness of the network is enough.

When a relationship is formed on a social media site, a node has been created in a network connected to other nodes with ties (i.e., connections). In a network, there is some relationship of at least one of the nodes to another. Ties are the relationships between the nodes. But for a network to occur, ties have to allow communication or influence of some sort.

Very few of the connections we have with others are symmetrical or completely equal. We see this inequality in social media. On Facebook, we have to accept the initial connection with someone before we are "friends." But once we've made that connection, either of us can edit our settings to prevent the other from seeing aspects of what we post. In Google Plus, we can add people to our "circles," and they don't have to add us back. The same is true of Twitter—someone can follow you without you having to follow him in return.

It's interesting that with circles in Google Plus, Google has introduced a new way to visualize the network. Facebook offers similar functionality, with the significant difference that in Google Plus, connecting with someone is the act of adding the person to a circle, whereas in Facebook, you connect with someone, then add her to a group.

The British psychologist Robin Dunbar made a remarkable observation: primate groups have a tendency to limit the number of others in their species with whom they interact. Dunbar wondered if there was a correlation between the size of a species' neocortex and those group sizes. Based on his calculations, he hypothesized that the maximum size for stable social networks for humans should be around 150 people. Since then, he has discovered that many societal groups in fact tend to follow that hypothesis. There is a great deal of confusion in the study of social media about what has come to be known as the Dunbar number. It doesn't mean that people can't have more than 150 friends, or that they can't really know more than 150 people. It does mean that it's pretty difficult for individuals in a group of more than 150 people to understand each one's relationship with all the others in the group, a hallmark of stable social networks.

A study by Indiana University's Bruno Goncalves found that the Dunbar number defined the pattern of how the majority of people use Twitter. While people may follow and be followed by thousands of people, the real dialogue tends to happen with a smaller subset of people. For the marketer, this might mean that if you are engaging in microaudiences and need your team to engage individuals, you might find that there is a threshold of how many people your team members can sustain personal relationships with.

Conversations

At one time, if a man had said he was having a "conversation" with a married woman, it could have landed him in trouble, for the term connoted sexual relations. If he was referring to a good chat he had with that woman, he'd have been better off to say they were having *intercourse*, although today the meanings have swapped places. We've come to think of the word *conversation* specifically to mean talking. If your boss tells you he wants to have a conversation with you, he might be implying that he has something to tell you that you don't want to hear, but usually, to have a conversation is a *pleasant* matter.

Today, having a conversation implies a give-and-take of ideas. We take turns. While that sounds simple, even the most mundane conversations can possess rich patterns and submessages. In the 1960s, sociologist Harvey Sacks studied the recorded telephone calls to a Los Angeles suicide hotline and in the process founded the discipline of *Conversation Analysis* (CA). In CA, conversations are analyzed for what is actually said, for pauses, and for what isn't said. What emerges from CA is that conversations are much more than a simple give-and-take, involving a complex negotiation and collaboration to get to the underlying meaning and purpose. Many statements require what's referred to as *repair* in CA. Sometimes we repair what we've just said, and often we repair what the other person has just said.

While CA was originally developed as a means to better understand oral communication, it also holds promise for the study of social media, which is proving to be a hybrid of the written and the oral. As more and more marketing efforts move from the realm of wholesale broadcast to that of one-on-one conversations, we might benefit from making CA part of our research.

Art Zeidman, president of Unruly Media, provided an illustration of how his organization looks at different messages for its subtext (Table 2.1).

TABLE 2-1 Social Triggers

	RATIONALE FOR SHARING	TEXT	SUBTEXT
Self-Validation: express yourself	Personality	"this is awsm! LOL!"	[This piece of content will show you my personality, e.g., GSOH, EMO, first in the know.]
	Passions	"Check this out! This'll be me at the weekend"	[This piece of content will show my passions, e.g, I love snowboarding, I love Justin Bieber, I love Seth Godin, I love my iPhone.]
	Projection	"Just seen this."	[This piece of content will show you that I have something to say; your response will show me someone is listening]

TABLE 2-1 Social Triggers, *continued*

	RATIONALE FOR SHARING	TEXT	SUBTEXT
Social Grooming: nurture relationships	Greeting	"saw this and thought of you"	[This piece of content of your home town/your favorite band/ celeb will prove that I know you, I understand you.]
	Belonging	"How cool is this?!"	[This piece of content will prove I'm like you, we have a shared experience, we are members of the same tribe, we share the same brand affinity or an oppositional brand loyalty.]
	Value	"you should deffo see this"	[This piece of content will prove I'm useful to you. I can tell you something that will make you smile/ help you out/give you kudos within the tribe.]
World Domination: build a following	Originality	"Scoop! You heard it here first."	[This piece of content will convince you I'm a valuable source of information and font of wisdom.]
	Influence	"Wow! 15k RTs is a new record for me"	[The response to this piece of content will convince you there are a lot of people listening to me, so perhaps it's time you did too!]
	Authority	"Something I pulled together with the team. Enjoy!"	[This piece of content will convince you I am authority in this area. I have access to the best people/ stats/data/insights.]

The ways in which people communicate seem to be endless. We sigh, state facts, cajole, whisper, demand, and laugh. Within the complexity of our use of words, though, the ways in which we do so seem to fall into some major categories.

Threaded conversations have been a mainstay of social media since the inception of the Internet. One of the earliest inventions was that of threaded discussions, particularly in bulletin boards. A person could start with a statement or question, and then others could comment or reply. In turn, others could attach commentary to the comment, creating a thread that would lead back to the original post. The Facebook wall, by contrast, is not a true threaded conversation, as people can only respond generically to the initial post, not specifically to comments without calling them out in particular.

It's interesting to see how the threading of conversations occurs differently on each of the major platforms. For instance, when a good friend in our marketing community passed away, a Facebook post became a place where people could leave their thoughts and memories. Twitter didn't lend itself to that sort of memorializing but instead provided the platform for quickly spreading the news.

Monologue: If you went to the grocery store and got yourself a soap box, you'd be foolish to stand on it in the town square and start espousing your opinions. First of all, the boxes are made of cardboard now, and surely the thing would collapse. Second, impromptu public oratory seems to have fallen into disfavor since the days of World War I. Nevertheless, you might get some feedback. The gathering crowd might boo, hiss, or "amen" in response to your words. Even if they stood in silence, that non-communication would be the basis of a dialogue between speaker and audience. Broadcast is modestly different, involving the use of some mechanical device to help amplify the message. But with broadcast, the audience give-and-take is missing. If I stand on a balcony with a megaphone, or with a microphone and PA system, I'm much less apt to hear my audience in return.

Dialogue: *Dialogue* originally meant a form of argument. If you want to bone up on your philosophy, you can read the Dialogues of Plato, although the form is said to have been extant even among the ancient Sumerians. *Discussions* were often part of judicial decisions, and today, they still have an air of seriousness about them. If the subject is frivolous, we have a good chat, although to chat online could mean to be having a discussion. Dialogue is found wherever we instant-message, private-message, or discuss. A fair amount of listening and reciprocity are hallmarks of dialogue.

Multilogue: In 1993 Gary Shank wrote a paper in which he suggested a new linguistic concept called the *multilogue*. In the multilogue, one person might initiate the conversation, but others might jump in and take it out of the originator's control. A lot of people can talk at once and still retain the distinctiveness of their own voices. Twitter chats strongly resemble a multilogue, with their extremely fast pace, making it impossible for any one person to keep up with all of the rapid-fire communication.

Direct messages may not exemplify social media, yet most social media platforms include the capability. Without direct messages, there wouldn't be the possibility of taking public conversations offline, which provides some freedom. The possibility that a third person is at least able to see your conversation shapes the dialogue, as people behave differently if they suspect that they are being watched.

Groups

Some social media sites start as special interest groups. Others allow for the forming of groups within the platform. Some platforms allow for the making of groups, while others are built on groups. On Twitter, people form their own groups simply through the use of a hashtag. Examples include the #usguys and #latism hashtags. I'll be discussing the remarkable power of how people work in groups in Chapter 8, "Chasing the Whales."

The terms *group* and *community* tend to be used interchangeably. M. Scott Peck, the well-known author and psychologist, described *community* as a group of people who have gone through several stages, emerging as a consensus-governed, nonexclusive group. Based on his workshops, Peck decided that real communities went through

- ▶ Chaos
- ▶ Emptiness
- ▶ True community

I wouldn't totally rule it out, but it seems unlikely that such a community would emerge from interactions that were entirely online. It's simply too easy for an unbounded group to slip in and out of the steps needed to form Peck's idea of community.

Another American psychologist, Bruce Tuckman, theorized that all groups go through several stages in their development:

- ▶ Forming
- ▶ Storming
- ▶ Norming
- ▶ Performing

and finally, because ostensibly a group forms in order to achieve something:

- ▶ Adjourning.

Do all groups form in order to achieve a goal? Or is it then a *team* we're speaking of?

In the nineteenth century, ethnologists used the term *affinity groups*, as did Spanish anarchists (*grupos de afinidad*), leading to the term being used to describe political groups. For ethnologists, the phrase related to their use of the word *affinity*, which inferred relationship by marriage or other ties as opposed to genetics. Another use of the word *affinity* means *liking*. We both might have an affinity for chocolate ice cream. Like the word *community*, the phrase *affinity group* has historically been used in many different ways within various disciplines.

Teams, of course, definitely have a common goal. They are organized for the purpose of fulfilling the goal and, after completing that goal, may go on to work toward another goal. Teams are typically organized in order to solve certain types of problems or to attain certain types of goals. The communities that I can think of might have common goals, but the goal is not necessarily the *raison d'être*. Often, their purpose is in living a certain lifestyle.

Social clubs, too, differ from communities. We might visit our social club on Tuesday night, play some poker, and recite some poetry, but then we return home. The social club might be *in* the community or outside—but in some form or another, it stands apart. In other words, with social clubs, we come together to socialize—just to be together and share some activities that we all like.

Where a platform supports group formation, the marketer should look to join groups or even create them when they don't exist. On the other hand, when a platform does not support group formation, other tactics should be used.

Gaming

Before my son became a teenager, I made games out of many unpleasant activities. Of course, he's on to me now, but before he became jaded, I could make a contest out of brushing our teeth a little bit longer or seeing who could be ready for bed the quickest. I was bringing gamification to tedious tasks. There are some interesting physiological and psychological powers at play when this is done. When people receive unexpected payoffs, a small increase in dopamine occurs. Dopamine is a brain chemical that tends to make you feel a lot better.

Social media in and of itself has a lot of elements that are intrinsically gamelike. The acquiring of friends (gaining points) and the receiving of "likes," "pluses," or "thumbs-up" are microrewards. Other gamelike elements we're seeing in social media include challenges, trophies, badges, and achievements. Then there are points, levels, leaderboards, and virtual goods. These gamelike elements foster game behaviors on the platforms.

Presence

The very action of messaging or updating says, "I'm here." Some platforms specifically allow you not only to make your presence known, but also to do so specifically in some physical place. *Location-based services* (LBSs) have become popularized with Foursquare as a part of Facebook and many other social platforms, although many people have concerns about the real-world threats of allowing others to know where they are. A location-based service could lead to your house being broken into or a stalker knowing when you're at the coffee shop. The website Please Rob Me (www.pleaserobme.com) purports to bring awareness to the idea that when you are announcing that you're somewhere, you're also announcing that you're *not* at home. On the other hand, an LBS can actually bring the online world into the offline world, allowing businesses with physical locations to interact with their online customers.

Being able to see when someone is online lets other users know that person is potentially available to chat or play. This could discourage *lurking*, which is what someone is doing when she is listening in on public conversations without actively participating.

Curation

The desire to curate what might be considered a personal museum is not new. In the Victorian age, clipping illustrations and pasting them into large blank books along with calling cards and other ephemera was quite the rage. People would even paste in locks of hair and flowers, creating repositories of personal memories that might have meaning only to the person creating the scrapbook.

I remember receiving articles clipped out of the newspaper from my grandmother, usually with a little note saying something like, "I thought this would be of interest." Before the Internet, when it was more common to send one another actual letters, people were sharing content. This impulse to share content is not new. There is an element of gifting to this curating, of saying, *I was thinking of you*. It could also be a way of bringing yourself to someone else's thoughts, asking him to think of you.

Reputation

Some social sites allow you to achieve some form of scoring, showing your status in the community or allowing you to assess another's reputation within the social channel. Often, what we're seeing in action is social proof, which I'll be covering in Chapter 8. An example of social proof in action can be seen in the community that exists on SEOmoz, a website dedicated to search marketing. Community members are given points when they contribute to the community through blogging, indicating whether they like something or not, or leaving a comment. A similar phenomenon is seen in gaming when users can attain points for their participation in the system.

Gifting

Gifting behavior is ubiquitous in social media. It isn't always obvious, but it abounds. When one person retweets another's tweet, recommends a book, or "likes" a post, there is an element of gifting. It should be recognized that not all gifting is benevolent. Gifting can be a way of asserting control or begging forgiveness. For marketers, it can be valuable to understand the different motives behind gifting. In Chapter 8, I'll address the influence of gifting and reciprocity.

APPLYING THE SOCIAL PYRAMID DIAGRAM

We can apply the social pyramid diagram to various social platforms (Figure 2.2). If a site is strong in a certain element, we'll shade the triangle black; if the site is less strong, we'll use gray. You might identify social media features that aren't in this pyramid or find that some of the features I'm focusing on just aren't important to you. For instance, some social platforms allow businesses to have a presence as an entity, while others do not. Modify the diagram to suit your needs.

Social media marketers should understand social media platforms and behaviors in terms of patterns. Analyze each platform using the pyramid, or modify it as needed. Seeing social media interactions in terms of patterns will help in the analysis of engagements so that you can assign value to those engagements.

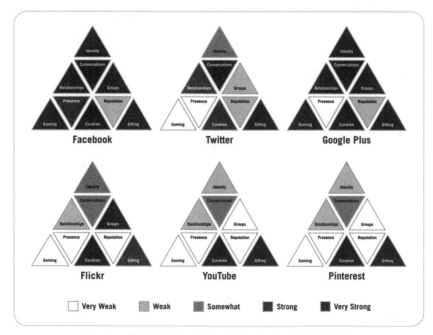

FIGURE 2.2 The social pyramid applied to six social platforms

The ideas about how many social media devices there are, and placing these into a graphic representation, evolved through the thinking of several individuals. I have modified these ideas to my own thinking.

One of the cofounders of the popular photo-sharing website Flickr, Stewart Butterfield, proposed that social platforms comprise five fundamental devices:

- ▶ Identity
- ▶ Presence
- ▶ Relationships
- ▶ Conversations
- ▶ Groups

A senior software applications developer at Yahoo!, Andrew Wooldridge, suggested two more:

- ▶ Reputation
- ▶ Sharing[4]

Information architect Gene Smith, borrowing from Peter Morville's visual device, a seven-element honeycomb for user experience, then proposed combining these seven devices into a graphic representation.[5] When I added the two more elements, the honeycomb no longer sufficed, as elegant as it was.

✔ CHECKLIST

☐ Apply the social pyramid diagram to the social platforms where your organization is active.

☐ Make note of which aspects you are fully using.

Consider taking greater advantage of the elements you're not using

☐ Identity

☐ Relationships

☐ Conversations

☐ Groups

☐ Curation

☐ Reputation

☐ Gifting

CHAPTER 3

HERDING CATS
MANAGING THE SOCIAL MEDIA TEAM

INTRODUCTION TO HERDING CATS

The phrase "herding cats" makes me laugh a little. Anyone who has ever owned a cat knows that they don't usually do tricks on command and are resistant to the normal ways we incentivize animals to perform for us. The phrase "herding cats" was popularized in reference to computer programmers, who tend to be fiercely independent. People who work in social media tend to invite the same reference, as we need them to be independent and to have smarts. Doing social media as a job is not burger flipping. But as in the world of programming, some approaches have emerged that enable us to direct a social media team in ways that result in the outcomes we need.

Interesting difficulties arise in managing social media marketing teams. Because of social media's newness, no one at this point has more than five to seven years' experience managing a social media team. Furthermore, it's likely that members of any given team have moved from one organization to another, facing very different challenges. Team members might have deep experience in public relations or marketing, yet the fundamental differences between the disciplines are likely to cause confusion. In short, this is a new "industry."

Processes for social media marketing have not become ubiquitous and are not fully developed in organizations. The roles and responsibilities for such teams are nascent and still undergoing refinement. The roles discussed in this chapter might be filled by just one person, or in a larger enterprise, by a whole team. Organizations can also use outsourced teams to fill all or some roles.

Some have argued that social media team members need to be internal employees, that given the nature of social media, people outside a company, such as vendors, aren't sufficiently intimate with the organization. However, I've seen enough examples of outsourced team members providing top-notch work that I'm of the mind that it is simply a different type of employee relationship. The important thing is that in some form or fashion, the outsourced people must be able to communicate with the internal people and get the information they need to do a great job. Extra attention needs to be given to keep the outside team informed about things that happen or change inside the company. At DragonSearch, we have weekly calls with companies for whom we do social media, enabling the various departments to share relevant developments.

ROLES AND RESPONSIBILITIES

Social media roles vary from organization to organization, as each has its own needs. These roles may be filled by one or several people. Overall, they fall into three main buckets: a leadership role, someone who is comfortable with high-level strategy and is capable of communicating clearly with senior leadership; community management roles that span both internal and external communities; and tactical roles, people who execute actual work within the social media platforms. Whoever fills the leadership role—whether it's a strategist, community manager, or chief marketing officer—needs to understand the world of business and the dynamics of the organization's particular industry and be able to translate the world of social media back to business stakeholders. The challenges are not unlike those that marketers have always faced in explaining the underlying value of brand management.

Affability and social intelligence are two of the most important characteristics for team members—people who have a real knack for being able to turn a friendly phrase, as opposed to one that is simply a reply. Social intelligence is the ability to understand one's own emotions and to empathize and respond appropriately to others. People with a high social IQ are smart in their relationships with others—they know how to sense another's feelings and respond appropriately. I'm not saying these are the only characteristics that are important, just that we've found them to be indispensable.

Social media marketing professionals don't grow on trees. Even someone who has gone through training or worked at another company will probably still need to learn how your company does social media. This means that instead of trying to find ("buy") people with professional social media experience, you'd do well to stay focused on the qualities that make a great social media professional and "grow" the needed skills.

Finding people who actually spend time in social media is a plus. Seek people who are literate. Social media is, after all, a form of literature. Some individuals possess an amazing capacity to be playful in social media. While playfulness may not be appropriate for all brands, the ability to live in an imagined space and to riff off the elements that encourage virtual tribes is of great value. One member of the DragonSearch team came to the company with a particularly charming writing style in which she creates narratives of action within her communications. For instance, she might write, "leans in closer to listen." When asked about where she acquired this style, she said it came from watching closed-caption television, where actions are often described along with the dialogue.

Social Media Team Roles

Director of social media (DSM). The director is responsible for providing the high-level strategy that the team will implement and is the most seasoned veteran of the social media team. Preferably, this individual will have experience in public relations, marketing, and marketing communications. The DSM should be up on the latest advances in social media and should have a deep understanding of the underlying patterns of social platforms.

Community manager. The community manager role will be described in more depth in Chapter 7. In some companies, this person doubles as the strategist and is at least at management level, able to discuss larger business strategies with executives and to communicate back to the C-suite the underlying reasons for engaging in social media in different ways. Often, the community manager also actively engages in social media, representing the brand, and helps to further the goals and objectives of the team's strategy and plan. It isn't uncommon for organizations to need their social team members to be available on weekends and in the evening. This is particularly true with community managers, who need to be able to respond quickly to arising issues. In a noted instance with the Red Cross that I'll be discussing later in the book, team members were on the phone with one another in the middle of the night in order to respond quickly to a miscommunication. Community managers must demonstrate an ability to be diplomatic and not overly quick to respond to what might be perceived as personal attacks. Great community managers practice a sort of social aikido, deflecting potentially volatile communications.

Zane Aveton's definition of community manager: Community managers are the personality and voice of your brand. They are also the thought provokers, the lovers, the approachable human aspect, the skillful responders, the salespeople so good at selling and driving campaign *buzz* that they are not selling at all—simply sharing the awesome. They are the strategic eyes and ears, the idea stimulators, the liaisons, the valuable connectors and the strategic alliance builders. They are knowledgeable content creators—equally skillful at discovering and curating content that what will keep all (the right) eyes attentively focused on your brand.

Blog editor. In many social media strategies, the blog takes on a central role. Blogs are an ideal platform to make use of the brains and talent both within and outside of the marketing team. The blog becomes the equivalent of a publication and requires editing and leadership in the same way that a publication does. The blog editor should have a thorough understanding of how the blog is categorized and tagged, a basic understanding of SEO, and know-how to guide writers in posting.

Blogger. Blogging constitutes a unique form of writing. Writers with extensive magazine or newspaper experience are not, by default, great bloggers. Certainly, a blogger should have experience with longer forms, but he or she should also be adept at web writing. Bloggers can be community managers in their own right, as the microcosm of the blog post can become an impromptu community. It's important that bloggers be able to nurture that space. In some industries, long, thoughtful, essay-like posts get the most commentary, while in other industries, posts that consist of nothing more than a photograph and a title get the most feedback. Whatever the case in your world, you will want a blogger who excels in communicating with your target audience.

Channel specialist. Larger teams often include specialists assigned to individual platforms. New platforms are being introduced weekly, along with updates to existing platforms. The channel specialist should know everything there is to know about her platform(s).

Channel monitor. Marcy Massura of Weber Shandwick recommends channel monitoring as a development role for community managers. A channel monitor keeps an eye on one or more channels and informs the community manager of opportunities such as trending topics, breaking news items, and important industry links. A channel monitor can also create pieces of communication to be vetted and distributed by the blogger or community manager.

Search engine optimization specialist. The integration of your social program with search engine optimization (SEO) can help drive a lot of new traffic to your website and can increase your influence within your areas of interest. Anyone and everyone creating content for the blog should be well versed in basic SEO tactics, and in an ideal world, anyone posting to your social media platforms should have an understanding of the important families of key phrases to use. It's also important that your social media profiles be optimized. While a full-time SEO specialist may not be necessary, you'll want someone on your team who possesses SEO optimization skills.

Photographer/videographer. This person should have an understanding of podcasting and vlogging (video blogging). Photos and videos can help a social media presence by breaking up the monotony of text and getting users engaged in new ways. A video can easily be transcribed, providing text as well, which in turn helps SEO. If your team can't support a dedicated photographer or videographer, get training and equipment for existing team players. Simply using a digital camera at an event provides a whole new chunk of potential content.

Web producer. Even though the social media team may not be responsible for in-depth maintenance of the website, it can be valuable to have someone on the team who can manage small changes. This person should have an understanding of HTML and CSS, the most prevalent coding used on websites.

Web analytics specialist. The analytics specialist needs to be able to navigate the tools used for pulling data about both the website and the various social channels. This person's understanding of data needs to go well beyond the default offerings of off-the-shelf tools. The analyst needs to know how to dig past the obvious metrics and get to underlying truths.

Knowledge and Training

Managers at every agency I've dealt with, from solo marketing teams to the largest interactive agencies, agree that their greatest challenge lies in continuous learning and sharing of knowledge across teams. Social media isn't changing annually, quarterly. or monthly; it's changing weekly, even daily. At one time, an individual could master enough of social media to be a stand-alone maven, but today that simply isn't feasible.

At many agencies, such as BlueGlass Interactive, Night Agency, and here at DragonSearch, "lunch-and-learns" are regular events where team members can share information about new social media changes. Every month, the Night Agency conferences with a partnering company in Brazil via a webcam so that the two companies can share information. If yours is a larger organization, consider bringing in people from different departments, and build programs around both giving and getting information from those other silos.

At lunch-and-learns and other training sessions, team members can provide workshops or presentations to the rest of the team or even to people outside the marketing department. By creating a calendar of such trainings, marketing team members can develop their own presentation skills and dig more deeply into their areas of expertise.

Leaders, community managers, and strategists should also receive training, as should individuals throughout the team. Areas of training to consider include

- Strategy, leadership, and culture
- Metrics and analytics (While you may have people whose main job is to analyze data, everyone on the team can benefit from being able to pull out relevant bits of information from whatever tools you are using.)
- Content development, management, and other methods related to engaging and moderating online conversations
- Interaction with particular social platforms

POLICIES AND PROCEDURES

Some norms will be embedded in your team's culture. They will feel natural, not worth documenting. But you have to remember, it's eminently easier to get a new team member up to speed if such norms *are* documented. Documenting procedures and policies will also enable your team to work more easily and quickly.

There may be two sets of policies: one for the enterprise, and one strictly for the marketing team. There is no reason to burden people outside of the marketing team with detailed policies that might be needed only in marketing. The marketing team will require more specifics, as they would have control over aspects of accounts and communications that others may not. For instance, a general member of the company may not have the ability to delete a public comment on a particular social platform, whereas a member of the marketing team could have that ability. Since the deletion of public comments can be incendiary, there should be a policy for the marketing team to handle that.

One of the best ways to continue improving processes is to keep documentation living and updated. Create an outline of the necessary processes, and build into the calendar periodic review dates. These reviews can be weekly ("Team, is there anything that stood out this week that would benefit from being a process or policy?"), or biannual. Put longer-cycle reviews on the calendar with an agenda.

Maintaining Records

Your organization might use an enterprise-level system for managing social media connections that will probably create a record of all of your social communications. You might also need to manually maintain a comprehensive "social media bible" in which you keep track of details, such as specific account information. Don't make the mistake of waiting until someone leaves your organization only to discover that no one else has access to a certain account.

Policies

A social media policy is a "must have" for all companies. The creation of such a policy provides employees clarity, reduces risk, and can actually be a big driver in communicating the brand with a virtual army of employees. A good social media policy will guide team members without someone standing over their shoulder telling them what to do.

There are thousands of examples of social media policies online, many belonging to reputable companies. In analyzing these policies, certain patterns emerge: The best policies are not so much proscriptions of "thou shalt nots" as they are true guides to help team members in questionable situations. They also help to affirm brand attributes.

Ideally, a social media policy is a living, breathing document, one that is updated periodically to meet new challenges. By calendaring social media policy reviews every 6 to 12 months, you can help to ensure that the system improves. In larger organizations, it makes sense to include a wide range of team members in policy review meetings.

Typical organizationwide policies[1] include

1. *Overall philosophy* characterizes the organization's general approach to social media, be it open and inviting, or restrictive.
2. *Employee access and acceptable use* addresses whether employees' access to social media will be restricted, completely open, or something in between. Are there limitations during working hours as opposed to nonworking hours? Keep in mind that in addition to the major social media platforms, there are blogs, discussion boards, and other social media that might be specific to any given person's job or the company in general.
3. *Account management* specifies who can create and control accounts in the organization or brand name. It isn't uncommon for a new social media platform to emerge and for Bob down in sales to start using it. A recent court case illustrates this need clearly: Noah Kravitz is being sued for $340,000 by his former employer, alleging that the Twitter account he built up to over 17,000 followers while employed at PhoneDog is a customer list.[2]
4. *Employee conduct* covers behavior in social media, including rules about online identities and policies regarding communications about other employees, vendors, and customers. These policies may also cover procedures for communicating with the press or with people who are being negative about the brand.
5. *Content policies* generally cover what content can and can't be posted in social media. These policies might also address issues of ownership. For instance, if an employee blogs during working hours, is that content owned by the company as a work for hire? Can employees request that content be removed when they leave the company?
6. *Security policies* typically mirror non–social media security policies but are still commonly stated.
7. *Legal issue* policies generally cover disclaimers, records management (particularly for industries or organizations that are subject to compliance laws), and copyright issues.
8. *Brand* policies cover the brand's voice and other brand attributes.

Troll Fighting

Many policies provide guidance for dealing with difficult people in social media, such as trolls (people who are looking to cause trouble and mayhem) and snarks (people who are negative).

The Air Force Blog Assessment diagram, developed by the Air Force Public Affairs Agency, provides a great process flow for responding to social media in general. This process is based on Assessment, Evaluate, and Respond. In the assessment phase, you determine whether the posting is positive, and, if not, ask the question, Is the person or site a "troll" (dedicated to bashing and degrading others), "rager" (rant, rage, joke, ridicule, or satirical in nature), "misguided" (erroneous facts in posting), or an "unhappy customer"? The Air Force's response depends on the type of post.

Marketing teams may need additional guidance in policy and procedures. At least two of the four great Twitter gaffes presented in Chapter 11 could have been prevented with procedural guidance, such as the use of different software for company and client accounts.

START WITH MONITORING AND RESEARCH

Every social media team member should know how to perform research at some level or another. By starting with research, each person learns about several pivotal elements that she will face when actually engaging in social media communications. The main research tasks include

- ► Keyword research
- ► Influencer research
- ► Competitive research
- ► Community research

After monitoring and research, individuals may participate in daily social communications. If circumstances allow, and if multiple people are involved with your social media efforts, you can have a "Scrum" meeting (explained later in the chapter) at the beginning or end of the day to review all of the day's communications. If only one person handles social media for your organization, a weekly meeting between that individual and the marketing manager will probably suffice.

Keyword Research

In keyword research, we're borrowing a play from the search engine optimization world, identifying how people are actually using words to satisfy their searches. In keyword research, we also expand our own vocabulary on a topic so that we have a better idea of the depth and breadth of a domain.

Keyword research begins with the development of a *seed list*, wherein information is gathered, typically through interviews with stakeholders. You can also analyze the websites of competitors to identify relevant words. Once the seed list is compiled, the words are run through a software service that expands on the list, providing alternative and related phrases. The free tools included in Google AdWords work well for this purpose. The end result is a much longer, more comprehensive list. Nonrelevant phrases are weeded out, and then the list is run through a traffic estimation tool, which is also available through Google AdWords. This will provide you with an understanding of the volume of search traffic for a particular phrase.

Keyword analysis helps us understand what phrases people are actually using (marketing teams are often guilty of hubris in thinking they know exactly which phrases matter), where on the web people are talking about relevant topics, and, finally, who is influential in the various social platforms.

Influencer Research

In the social media process I outline in this book, we move from microsegmentation (finding the smallest possible groups that are important to your topic), to finding the communities that those people are in, to identifying the people who are influential in those communities. Another approach is based on topics: identifying topics of importance based on keyword research, and then identifying the people who are influential for those topics. In either method, keyword research and web-based search is used to identify the individuals.

Several third-party tools have been developed to assist in identifying influencers, such as Kred, Klout, and PeerIndex. Some of the enterprise social media management tools also have built-in influence tools, but Google is, in itself, our favorite research tool. If someone is influential across various social channels, it's likely he'll also appear in search results. In a comparison test we did on the keywords "physical therapy," the topmost candidate from search-based research had an active blog that averaged over 10 unique commenters per post, while the topmost influence-tool candidate had a modest Twitter following and a blog that was not well attended. Ultimately, we determined that the dialog on Twitter around that individual was not as significant as the other candidate's blog comments.

Competitive Research

One of the greatest challenges facing organizations or brands that are coming late to social media is gaining a strong foothold in communities where a competitor is already well established— particularly if the competitor created the social space. The site colourlovers.com is an online community for all things having to do with color, developed by the makers of software for color matching and palette creation. While the site is an open forum and other color product manufacturers can participate, the products listed on the top menu belong to the host company.

By using search or tools like Radian6 or Sysomos, it is simple to discover where your competitors are active in social media. In creating a competitive brief, you might even uncover unexpected topics with which your competitors are active.

Community Research

There are two aspects to doing research on communities. The first is finding relevant communities. Again, keyword research will help. In some cases, you have to find communities that may not be available to the search engines, in which case you might need to use other research tools and research other third-party sources. For instance, you might be looking for a community that deals specifically with a particular cancer. The community is closed but is in itself discussed on the web and can be identified through search engines. The second aspect of community research is the study of actual conversations in those communities, often referred to as online ethnography or netnography.

SOCIAL MEDIA RUGBY

In 1986, a paper by Hirotaka Takeuchi and Ikujiro Nonaka describing a new approach to product development appeared in

Harvard Business Review. Unlike conventional product development projects that operated like a relay race (separate groups of people doing different parts, then handing them off to the next group), this approach was more like a rugby team running down the length of the field, the entire team sticking with the project from start to finish.

One of the salient features of this approach was the idea that leadership should establish the big-picture vision, allowing the team to determine the best ways to attain the desired result. This is a salient point in Toyota's philosophy, as well as in the military strategy philosophy of John Boyd.

The approach was later adapted to Agile software development and dubbed *Scrum*, which is the word used to describe how rugby games are restarted after an infraction. While conceived of and created for software development, Scrum is adaptable and relevant to social media marketing teams. Basically, very large overall desired outcomes are thought of in small chunks. Those small chunks are conceived of and communicated to the team in terms of stories, at which point the team determines the effort required and works to enact the story.

Social Media Scrum

Scrum and social media marketing were made for one another. In Scrum, emphasis is placed on self-organized teams without hierarchy. Social media is characterized by an ethic of transparency and a closer intimacy between people. In Scrum, instead of "events," there are "ceremonies."

At the same time, though, Scrum was designed for software—and there are many aspects that aren't a great fit for social media marketing. Where that's been the case, there are variations on how we use Scrum for social media, which I'll point out as we go along. In some cases, I use different words to describe analogous roles or activities in Scrum for software development, not simply for the sake of being different but because those words carry a different tone in marketing and the social media process benefits from its own vocabulary.

Social media projects take many different forms. As an agency for outside brands, we at DragonSearch typically design social media projects to fit the constraints of a budget. Brand teams have their own constraints as well based on the resources available to the marketing team.

It's easy, particularly in a brand management project, to lose sight of goals and objectives. Bringing the Scrum process into play helps the team keep measurable objectives in mind at all times and to push the envelope with activities that are delivering results versus activities that are ineffective.

There are a few moving parts to Scrum for social media marketing, but after you've absorbed them, you'll realize that it is a powerful way to organize the work. There are three major roles of note: the Master Strategist (called the Product Owner in traditional Scrum), the Scrum Master, and the Team Member.

The Master Strategist represents the organization and, ultimately, all of the people who will derive value from interacting with the brand. The first task is to create an overarching game plan. Since the social media world is changing quickly, it makes sense to create a *Big Game Plan* for six months to a year.

The Big Game Plan

In the Big Game Plan (BGP, also called the Meta Scrum), you should revisit the big vision and goals of the organization. There can be some big sweeping statements here in regards to social media. For instance:

▶ When people talk about soft drinks at soccer games, we want them to be talking about Acme Fizzle.
▶ We want to increase awareness of our brand in our target market by 10 percent.
▶ We want a 20 percent increase in online sales.

You can then begin to map out what it would take within the social world to achieve those goals.

The planning in the BGP can be broken down into smaller chunks of two to three months. These smaller game plans should map to the larger plan. At this point, you can now create a *Product Backlog*, or, if you prefer, the *Master Backlog*. This is a document, whiteboard, or any other large area where you can post.

Master Backlog

The Master Backlog is made up of *stories* (*user stories* in software Scrum). Stories are brief concise statements usually in this form:

"As a (*role*), I want (*goal/desire*) so that (*benefit*)."

For example:

"As *head of marketing*, I want *at least 20 big influencers to share our thought pieces with their communities* so that *potential clients doing their due diligence can see that we are credible.*"

"As *a marketer*, I want *a steady group of 10 people outside of the company commenting on each blog* so that *our company is a central part of the discussion around blue widgets.*"

"As *a marketer* I want *our Facebook friend count to be at least 10,000* so that *our social media presence has credibility.*"

Another approach is to think of the role in terms of people out there in the world and the value that your social media efforts can bring to them. This is where we can drill into those subsegments that we brainstormed:

"As a *Scottish Terrier fancier* I want *interesting blog posts to read every day* so *that I can indulge in my passion* resulting in *my thinking of Acme Dog Figurines when I'm buying gifts.*"

Important things to remember in writing stories include the following:

▶ Keep the stories concise. If they're too complicated, break them down into multiple stories.
▶ Be able to measure and test the story. Something vague, like "I want to be popular," would be difficult to test. "I want to be listed as the most popular site on Technorati" would be measurable.
▶ Make sure the story passes the Goldilocks test. If it's too small, it may not deserve to be a story; instead, lump it in with other microtasks. Likewise, if the story is too large, break it down into smaller stories. In Scrum, there is actually a word for a large story that contains smaller stories: *an epic.*

SOCIAL MEDIA SPRINTS

A Sprint is a chunk of work. The Sprint could be for particular objectives (e.g., "we are doing a lead-generation project around a coupon on Facebook") or for several objectives. Frequently, in our work, we may have several activity tracks proceeding simultaneously, such as when we're building connections, engaging in external communities, and cultivating our own blog community.

Sprint Planning Meeting

Assuming that clear long-term goals and objectives have been documented and communicated to the team, a Sprint planning meeting would take place to plan out the objectives of a shorter period of work. Exactly how long you want to plan for is up to you—there are not exact rules—but we recommend starting out with one- or two-week Sprints. Sprints can be planned around product releases, events, or other major organization milestones, or simply based on other stories that are created.

Time-box effort. The concept of the time-box is to give a time constraint to any effort, whether it's a meeting or a chunk of work. Agencies usually are more naturally adept at this, since they are often working within a budgeted time constraint. This means that if a meeting is set to be 30 minutes, it will stop after 30 minutes no matter what. If I have given myself two hours to respond to blog comments, then I will stop after two hours. The thinking here is that by setting a time constraint, I'm less apt to try to multitask and more apt to stay focused on the task at hand.

Prioritizing tasks. Prioritizing, or just ordering tasks, is a basic element of Scrum. What you use as a driving force in prioritizing is up to you—it might be value to a customer, or it might be the likelihood of a task contributing to achieving desired outcomes. Often, the discussion of why one task is more important than another reveals important information to team members.

Feedback loops. Feedback loops can exist at many levels: the highest level is where we review our big-picture strategy effectiveness, and the lowest level, our daily reviews. The daily reviews let us know how effective our work was during the day and give us a chance to discuss changing tactics if our work wasn't effective. There is also a middle-level looping that in Scrum naturally occurs at the end of any Sprint. For example, we might have a larger strategy that is based on a blog, but over several weeks, the programming team hasn't been able to launch the new blog. By considering this, we can adjust our stories to meet the changes. The potential win here is in creating a culture and mindset of constant and looping review of strategy and tactics at different levels, and at any natural review point.

Burndown. In traditional Scrum, burndown charts are used to show the progress of work within a Scrum. In social media, our efforts may not be output-focused, and thus a burndown chart may not be as effective. Where there is a clear output, though, a chart showing daily progress is an effective tool.

Daily Scrum

The Daily Scrum is a brief (15 minutes) meeting where each team member tells the group what she accomplished in the prior day and what she's setting out to accomplish today. Team members also share any impediments that they've encountered, providing the group with the opportunity to offer solutions. These meetings aren't just called standing meetings because they are regularly on the calendar but because everyone is expected to stand up. By actually standing up, people are less apt to make small talk or comments that don't add value to the meeting.

One project manager I spoke with told me that sometimes team members worked from home and would call in to the Scrum meeting. He insisted that he could tell if people weren't standing: there was just a little less urgency and more of a tendency for the conversation to wander.

MANAGING ACTIVITIES

There are many ways to divide up social media work depending on the larger objectives. If you're doing influencer work, the activities might be focused on the influencer list and keeping up with what those individuals are doing. If the focus is on community building, then the activities are going to be completely different.

Assigning Tasks

The last thing you want to do is create busywork for people. Therefore, request and expect tangible activity reports at the end of each day (or week, depending on which cycle works best for your team) for a particular endeavor. In doing so, you help to ensure focus on results and that the task is accomplished. If you're using a software system for managing all of your social media activities, this type of reporting can be automated. Otherwise, a web-based form can easily be created. Another option is to hand out clipboards with a simple blank form for each day like the one shown in Table 3.1.

TABLE 3.1 Daily Task Log

Date: Aug. 2, 2012	Team Member: RD Project: Acme Influence
PLATFORM	ACTION
Facebook	friended Danny Sullivan
Facebook	mentioned Danny Sullivan in wall post
Facebook	friended Mary Rose Smith
Facebook	friended Fred Jacobs
Blog	commented on http://www.dragonsearchmarketing.com/blog/metrics
Blog	commented on http://outspokenmedia.com/seo/what-to-look-for-when-hiring

Passwords and Security

Social media marketing teams are often working within dozens of different platforms, each with its own account names and passwords. These passwords need to be maintained in such a way that they can be changed immediately if an employee leaves the organization. Under no circumstances do you want an employee creating an account for the organization using his own information.

Make sure that passwords and account names are kept in one place that is accessible by upper management or HR. If an employee departs, the main passwords should be changed as a matter of policy and all accounts updated as necessary.

✔ **CHECKLIST**

Roles

Depending on the size of your social media team, consider the various roles which you might fill:

- ☐ Director of social media (DSM)
- ☐ Community manager
- ☐ Blog editor
- ☐ Blogger(s)
- ☐ Channel specialist
- ☐ Channel monitor
- ☐ Search engine optimization specialist
- ☐ Photographer/videographer
- ☐ Web producer
- ☐ Web analytics specialist

Policies

- ☐ Consider having these policies as stand-alone policies or as part of a larger policy.
- ☐ Overall philosophy
- ☐ Employee access and acceptable behavior policy
- ☐ Account management policy
- ☐ Employee conduct policy
- ☐ Content policy
- ☐ Security policy
- ☐ Legal issue policy
- ☐ Brand policy

CHAPTER 4

ENVISIONING RESULTS

FOCUSING ON DESIRED OUTCOMES

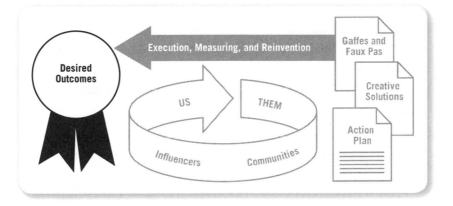

SOCIAL MEDIA AND THE ORGANIZATION

In interviews and discussions with social media leaders in dozens of companies and agencies, one message I heard repeatedly is that social media, even marketing in general, is too often implemented without strong ties to organizational vision, goals, and objectives. Marketers need to maintain vigilant focus on desired outcomes.

As marketers, we might belong to an organization where values and purpose are driving forces, or we might belong to an organization that is more focused on next quarter's financial returns. If we're fortunate enough to belong to the former, our social media work can become a contributing factor to the organization's bigger purpose. If we're less fortunate and belong to the latter, we might be able to play a role in helping the organization uncover larger meaning or at least help map a sense of purpose to business metrics.

We all know social media is changing marketing. We know it's changing customer relations, product development, human resources, and other key areas. We know we need to be doing it. But we're often unsure of the bigger picture, or how we're going to create real sustaining value. In marketing in general, we need a clear understanding of what we want to accomplish. If we jump in and start activities without first tying them to organizational goals, we won't even know when and if we're succeeding. Answering the question, "What is it we're trying to do here?" often just isn't enough. We need to map out a full picture of desired outcomes.

> In order to succeed a man must have imagination. He must definitely see in the near or distant future the perfect thing which he wishes to obtain. He must *imagine* the ultimate results of his endeavor.
>
> —E. St. Elmo Lewis

In order to clarify the language I'll be using to discuss desired outcomes, I offer the model shown in Figure 4.1. In this model, we move from vision, to goals, to objectives, and finally to specific metrics. In vision, we start out with the least specific and fuzziest notions and, with each step, move toward more specificity.

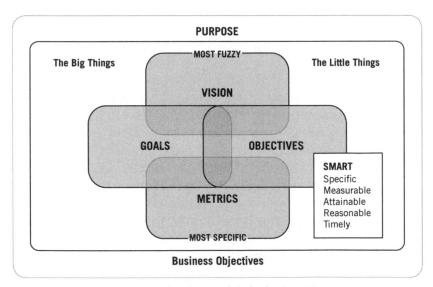

FIGURE 4.1 Landscape of desired outcomes

--------------------------------- **VISION** ---------------------------------

The popularization of the term *desired outcome* and the use of the word *vision* in business came about in the 1920s. Whereas *desired outcomes* first gained prominence in the literature of education, the word *vision* took hold in the literature of fraternal clubs and business organizations that had a strong evangelical influence, such as the Rotary, Kiwanis, Optimist, and Lions Clubs. Trace it back, and you can actually see a correlation between the abolition movement's use of *vision* and its subsequent use in the business world. For instance, the community perspective in Coca-Cola's current value statement was preceded by those early civic groups' focus on improving their communities.

In 1945, social psychologist Kurt Lewin established the Group Dynamics Research Center at MIT and introduced the thinking that in the 1950s would be the basis for the discipline of organizational development (OD). OD work frequently included the concept of vision into organizational change efforts. After all, in order to get unstuck from institutionalized behavior, people need to share a vision of something better, something more meaningful. Teams need to have a larger common purpose to rally behind. Since the spread of OD, the idea that businesses should have a vision, a mission, values, and purpose has become ubiquitous in leadership and management thought.

Vision is the pie in the sky. Those early abolitionists envisioned a world wherein all people treated one another as equals. One goal was the abolition of slavery. In business, we have two visions: the company vision that comes from the organization's leadership and drives the company's larger agenda, and the marketing team's vision, which should be in alignment with the organization or brand vision. Sometimes it's a play between the two. Vision should be grand as well as fuzzy, and possibly even audacious.

Perhaps my vision is for people to laugh. I want people to overcome their limitations and do things they never dreamed possible. Vision might be something that seems impossible but not so much so that it fails to inspire.

Many organizations use vision statements as overall guides to everything they do. At Coca-Cola, the vision is divided into different parts, addressing the vision of people, portfolio, partners, planet, and profit, and includes lines like, "Be a responsible citizen that makes a difference by helping build and support sustainable communities." Similarly, Pepsi's vision statement says, "Our vision is put into action through programs and a focus on environmental stewardship, activities to benefit society, and a commitment to build shareholder value by making PepsiCo a truly sustainable company."

Vision is so much larger than a goal. Once we've attained our goal, we must acquire a new goal, as a goal has an end in sight, a light at the end of the tunnel. A vision, on the other hand, can encompass many goals. I'm not saying we shouldn't have goals— goals are critical in our marketing efforts—but let those goals be enfolded in larger vision.

As business philosophy developed in the last century, a consensus emerged around the core elements of vision, values, and mission. Unfortunately, these same elements have been bandied about to the point where mentioning them instantly invokes dozens of Dilbert cartoons lampooning what has become trite and meaningless. That leaves us with a problem because vision, values, and mission are just as important as ever. They bring cohesiveness to business actions, provide teams with focus, and act as a heuristic or innate set of rules guiding bigger actions.

Values are what you hold sacred. What would you leap into the fire to save? Without values, you wouldn't feel that you were still you. They are in your DNA. The Declaration of Independence began with a statement of values. Values provide us with what I call passion points—things that our organization's leadership and culture get behind passionately and that allow us to connect with people.

The importance of values becomes even more pronounced in social media marketing, where great agility is needed. The individuals working for a brand need a framework. American fighter pilot John Boyd became one of the most famous military strategists of the late twentieth century. Focusing on the problem of how smaller, less-equipped armies often prevailed over larger, better-equipped forces, he devised a concept called the OODA Loop. OODA stood for observe, orient, decide, act. The loop part implies that it is a recurring process. Success depends on being able to work within your OODA Loop at a faster pace than your opponents. Boyd's thinking was focused on warfare, but people have applied his ideas to business as well. While seemingly simplistic, many aspects of Boyd's philosophy are worth consideration.

In studying the blitzkrieg, the German method of warfare that enabled the Germans to overrun the Maginot Line at the beginning of World War II, Boyd noted that the success worked from what was called the *Schwerpunkt*, a German word meaning "hard point." The *Schwerpunkt* implies a focus, or any concept that gives direction to our activities. Those at the top are tasked with setting the culture and agenda and then empowering people to do their job. The opposite of this is Command and Control (often abbreviated as C2), where decisions go through a hierarchical tree, often leading to decision and "analysis paralysis."

When organizations are able to tap into their bigger vision and values, they're working with their passion points. Passion points allow a company like Nike to focus on sharing a message about people transcending their physical limits to achieve great accomplishments. Passion points allow a company like Maxwell House to create a whole marketing campaign around the concept of optimism[1] and the Coca-Cola Company to send several bloggers on a worldwide trip to document how different people express happiness.

By having clearly articulated passion points, marketers can focus on communications that people will want to be a part of. In the process, the brand's association with those values will be stronger, and the sense of brand personality will flourish.

Having vision means keeping your eyes on the horizon. And if you've ever been sailing, you might know that the best way to prevent seasickness is to keep your eyes on the horizon. Social media can be likewise disorienting.

There is a tremendous power in being able to look at a piece of land, envision a beautiful building, and then see a building project through to completion. Usually, vision is not filled with details; it is the person seeing the world through the rose-tinted glass of "what can be." Vision is powerful in that it rallies support. Martin Luther King's dream was that people would be judged by the content of their character and that children of all colors would be able to play together: he kept to the broad brushstrokes. The same is true of the United States Constitution. Tremendous things have been accomplished, often preceded by an individual with a strong vision. This *Field of Dreams* approach has been cited in reference to Martin Luther King, Kennedy's intent to put men on the moon, and even the creation of the Internet. By having a clearly articulated vision, you can help drive your social media team to do things that go beyond the mundane. It can't simply be a vision of revenue growth or increased fans.

GOALS

A tremendous amount of confusion exists about the difference between goals and objectives. Many popular business writers now are saying that goals are longer term and fuzzier, while objectives are succinctly measurable. Texts from the 1960s say quite the opposite—that objectives are timeless and goals are measurable.[2]

Influential business thinker and consultant Peter Drucker introduced management by objectives in his 1954 classic *The Practice of Management*. Drucker himself doesn't discern between goals and objectives, but he does establish the popular conception of there being many objectives that may need to be attained before reaching a goal. In this sense, it could be seen more as an issue of granularity.

One way of designing goals for marketing purposes is to pull out the marketing funnel and see if there are places where you need to impact the larger organizational goals. In 1904, the editor of the magazine *Salesmanship*, Frank Hutchinson Dukesmith, introduced the concept that prospective customers go through stages of attention, interest, desire, and, finally, conviction. Over the years, this framework has morphed into attention, interest, desire, and action, providing the handy acronym AIDA. Later, in the late 1950s, Dukesmith's idea was conceptualized as a funnel, providing the sales funnel, marketing funnel, or customer funnel. If you understand that customers go through phases in their relationship to your company, it could help you use the right communication at the right time. When Dukesmith devised his steps, there wasn't even an endeavor called marketing; that was to come later, in the 1920s, when marketing was finally introduced to business school curricula.

The marketing funnel has come under quite a bit of criticism for being too simplistic, but it still has value as a high-level mapping device. Of its many variations, the one we've found to be most useful is

- ► Awareness
- ► Interest (consideration)
- ► Desire
- ► Action (the buying point)
- ► Satisfaction
- ► Advocacy

While social media has the greatest impact on the two ends of the funnel (awareness and advocacy), it can also be effective in the interim steps, particularly as more and more consumers use online search and social media to do homework (due diligence) on products and services.

Thinking in Phases

Once, presenting a marketing plan to a client, I said something about an issue being addressed in phase 2. The client blurted out, "I don't want to hear about 'phase 2'—every time we do a project, people are talking about these other phases that we don't ever seem to get to!'" When a plan spans two or more years, it can be easy to forget the bigger plan, which can also change.

Creating Value for the Customer

Your boss calls you into her office and asks you to take a seat. She tells you that the company needs to increase sales by 20 percent during the next year. Or she tells you that the company needs to increase its base of new customers by 10 percent. Or, gee, she suggests you use that new social media platform to sell more widgets.

The problem with this mindset is that customers don't care whether your overall revenue increases, if you have more customers, or if you sell more widgets. It doesn't even figure into their lives. It's true that if you make more profit, you'll plow more back into research and development and come up with a whole line of new products that do bring value to the customer. But really, it isn't the customers' job to work through all of that or even to trust that you will eventually provide them with more value. Customers need value now.

Lean, the business philosophy that came out of the work of W. Edwards Deming and the Toyota Production System, has as a core tenet that all of our activities should create value for the customer. Though the philosophy is typically associated with manufacturing, some companies are endeavoring to practice *lean marketing*. To do so means, of course, that every step of the marketing effort should create customer value, and that any step that doesn't is wasteful. What this means for setting vision and goals is that the customer vantage point should be paramount.

Another business philosophy that could be useful is that of the Balanced Scorecard, a strategic planning tool made popular by Robert S. Kaplan and David P. Norton. A core belief in the Balanced Scorecard is that financial indicators are important, but they are a lagging metric. The company should also be constantly measuring the learning and growth perspective, the internal process perspective, and the customer perspective. In looking at the Balanced Scorecard, I'm not suggesting that it is the role of marketing to drive the strategic planning process for the enterprise, but only that there are more ways of determining marketing value. Marketers should have these concepts at their disposal if they are going to better communicate the value of social media to stakeholders.

It might be that your organization does not harbor a mindset of customer value and that your big goals and vision have been set from above with a company-centric viewpoint. The challenge then for marketing is pairing that organizational viewpoint with the customers' world to find the common ground. You can still set a broader vision for your social media team.

While the big-picture vision should be at the top of everyone's page from the get-go, you can hold off on creating the goals if you're just initiating a social media marketing program. There is, after all, a lot of work to be done in getting accounts set up and starting the process of connecting and engaging. But after a month or two of being in the stream, identify those big goals. Once you have those big goals, you need to

▶ Make sure they're clear to all team members.
▶ Make sure management buys in and supports marketing efforts.

OBJECTIVES

While there may be confusion between goals and objectives, one useful concept that emerged from business thinking in the 1970s is SMART. SMART is an acronym for:

Specific and clearly stated
Measurable and based on data
Attainable and realistic
Relevant
Time-bound

George Doran, who introduced SMART, referred to SMART goals and objectives, but since then, many people refer simply to SMART objectives. While each point of SMART is relevant to the points made in this book, the most salient is that social media efforts are measurable. By keeping this in mind, you will develop a culture wherein every person on the marketing team will be thinking of metrics at all times. While an effort may arise every now and then that falls more into the "skunk works" category, the majority of work will be thought of in terms of measurability.[3]

CONVERSIONS IN SOCIAL MEDIA

For over 2,000 years, well into the seventeenth century, practitioners of alchemy endeavored to find the elixir of eternal life, the panacea, and the philosopher's stone. With the latter, supposedly, the basest of metals could be transmuted into the higher metals like silver and gold. This was, perhaps, the ultimate conversion. As marketers, we're not interested in converting things of higher value into things of lower value—we deal in the creation of value.

Value is a funny notion. If we find a person crawling across an arid desert on the brink of death by dehydration, we could probably sell that person a bottle of water for any price. That same bottle of water back at the corner grocery store could only be sold for the going price. So in other words, value is contextual.

Were we to offer our starving desert-crosser a Rembrandt painting in exchange for that bottle of water, he would decline. In that context, the bottle of water has more value than the painting. To further complicate the concept of value, imagine that back at the museum where the painting actually belongs, the leading expert should walk in one day and declare the painting a fake. It is the exact same painting that crowds of museum visitors were jostling to see just the day before, but now no one is interested, and the museum would be fortunate to receive a mere $10,000 for the piece at auction. What happened to the value? In this case, the value is a mental construct that has been altered by the new revelations about its authenticity.

There are many overall metrics and specific conversion actions to be considered:

1. Transaction—actually getting someone to add herself to our mailing list or even to purchase a product right in a social media channel. This conversion most closely aligns with conventional conversions.
2. Social proof. I'll be discussing social proof as an element of influence a bit later. This is where someone "likes," retweets, comments, or somehow takes an action that others can see and feel compelled to join the bandwagon.
3. Influencer actions. If we are employing an influencer strategy, any action an influencer takes that references our brand can be considered a conversion.
4. Share of voice. How often is Coca-Cola referenced as opposed to Pepsi or RC Cola (or any other soft drink for that matter) in discussions where soft drinks are mentioned? This is the share of voice.
5. Engagement. Engagement is difficult to measure, but we know it when we see it. The difficulty of measuring engagement is that it is like trying to measure the relative merits of one hug over another.
6. Amplification. When people share our content with others, our voice becomes amplified. It may be an overall goal to see our messages amplified, although this might also be tied in with an influence program and seen more in light of how much influence we are exerting. To what end are we exerting influence?
7. Being liked. Being liked is also a key component of influence and thus might be part of an influence program. Likability can be difficult to measure.

One of the challenges with social media is that many of the objectives that we can achieve map obliquely, not directly, to business objectives. It's as though we have to map one world to another—like, say, mapping the world of *Star Trek* to the world of *Star Wars*. They aren't just two different stories but, in our minds, two different realities. It's our job as marketers, though, to map one to the other so that we can more fully communicate with the C-suite.

Intentionality

Japanese calligraphy students are often asked to create an *enso*, a circle drawn with a single brushstroke. The calligraphy master can purportedly see into his student's mind with that single drawing. If the intention is to impress, that will be communicated. Intention communicates.

In business, we're out to make money. Coca-Cola might say that its purpose is to make people happy, but at the same time, its marketing objective is to double sales by the year 2020. Nike's goal is to help athletes realize their potential, but it's also to create value for shareholders. It's natural for businesses to have dual sets of goals and objectives for different stakeholders.

In our social media endeavors, we must lead with the nonfinancial goals, as financial goals are fundamentally anathema to the social ecosystem.

> The key to social media success is often being stubborn with your vision, but flexible with your plan.
>
> —Erik Qualman[4]

Urgency

John Kotter, the business thinker and writer, postulated that several steps are necessary to create sustainable change. The very first step is the *communication of urgency*. In creating your organization's social media marketing vision, what is urgent? What *must* change?

Businesses often create vision statements to guide the business. I'm suggesting that you should do so for your social media marketing efforts as well. Of course, the marketing vision statement should be related to the organization's overall vision and goals.

Create a social media marketing vision statement that paints a picture of how the organization's social media marketing is going to look at some point in the future—say, in three years. (Can we even imagine what social media will look like in the more distant future?)

> Acme Corporation will be a noticeable and outstanding feature in the online discussion of (*passion point*) to the point where everyone in the online space talking about (*passion point*) will be aware and see Acme Corporation in a positive light.

But don't just create a formal document according to a formula. Pull out the vision: in the ideal world, what would our relationship be with the world if we were able to all get in one room, have coffee, and chat?

> Learning what to want is the most radical, the most painful, and the most creative art of life.
>
> **—Sir Geoffrey Vickers**

Channel-Specific Vision

You can also create a vision specific to each social media platform. For instance, we can create a vision for how we would like our organization to be experienced on Facebook. A step in developing that vision could be to document what competitors are doing, or other businesses that might be considered leaders. Document all of the salient features of a given platform, such as:

- ▶ Follower size
- ▶ Inbound communications
- ▶ Microgifting by us
- ▶ Microgifting by our community
- ▶ User experience of page(s)

These aspects of what we'd like to get out of a particular social platform can be listed in a spreadsheet like the one shown in Table 4.1, with parallel columns where we document what the experience is like today, thus creating the basis for a gap analysis.

TABLE 4.1 Sample Facebook Goals Spreadsheet

	CURRENT	ONE-YEAR GOAL
Follower size	55,777	150,000
Inbound communications	16 items posted by others on our wall per day	50 posts by other per day
Microgifting by us	12 likes per day	75 likes per day
Microgifting by our community	15 likes per day average	55 likes per day average

Further aspects to consider are traffic from the social platform back to your site, how often your page is referred to by others, and so on. You might also have additional, more intangible aspects to your vision, such as wanting to see your presence on this particular social platform be so notable that it is cited in industry literature or talked about in the popular press.

Goals Document

Design and plan all of your projects on your desired outcomes—the vision, goals, and objectives you identified in that earlier phase of the process. If you adopt the Scrum method of project management, it will come naturally: run your desired outcomes through the lens of what the desired outcomes are for your customers or audience. *We* want to accomplish this, and *they* want that. Can we marry these two things together and have outcomes that fit both them and us?

With the goals in mind, map activities to the goals that will provide measurable outcomes. As Todd Wilms of SAP said, "Once you take it back to that initial step—'what is it that you're trying to accomplish?' then the measurements become really straightforward and there are two or three that you always want to look at. You're starting to tell a story with what social media does for your activity. You know, 'what are you trying to accomplish?' and 'What's the story you want to tell?'"

This is quite different from saying, "Let's do a whole bunch of activities, then measure what we're able to." There is a bias toward using the metrics that are easily available. It's our job as marketers to keep our eye on the big goals. By putting our desired outcomes into story terms, we're able to brainstorm actions that will fulfill that story and then measure the results back to those original desired outcomes.

> When you focus on what works and you dream of the possibilities, it's very inspiring to people.
>
> **—Bob Stiller,** Green Mountain Coffee Roasters

A table similar to Table 4.2 can easily be created wherein we place our goals, the activities that we believe will fulfill those goals, and the objectives and metrics required to achieve those goals.

TABLE 4.2 Mapping Activities to Goals with Measurable Outcomes

GOALS	STRATEGIES	TACTICS	METRICS
Grow the engaged Facebook fan base by 15% over 3 months	Engage with current fan base	Post 1–2 times per day: nonpromotional, passion-based topics	• Percentage growth of fan base number of engagements • Quality of engagements
		Post once per day: brand-related images, video, new product, event, press release, etc.	• Sentiment of engagements • Growth of mentions and others sharing our stuff
		Ask and answer questions to engage	• Growth of traffic to website from Facebook
		Use blog to create and share great content with fans	• Quality of traffic: time on-site, pages per visit, bounce rate
		Monitor and respond to engagements daily	• Conversions on website from Facebook traffic
	Connect with target audiences	Create an audience segmentation document	
		Connect with the different segments	
		Find who's already talking about the brand	
		Find influential blogs in each audience segment and engage with the community there	
		Share audience's posts, etc.	
	Provide exclusive offers for current fans	Create landing page on the website	
		Run promotions on Facebook, website, offline, and on other channels online to create buzz	
	Connect with organizations we already have a relationship with	Publications/media we already advertise with	
		Organizations or individuals our business collaborates with	

✔ CHECKLIST

Audit to be sure your organization has
- ☐ Clearly articulated vision
- ☐ Vision statement, goals statements, objectives
- ☐ Clear understanding on the part of all team members

CHAPTER 5

AWAKENING THE BRAND
HUMANIZING IT WITH
PERSONALITY AND VOICE

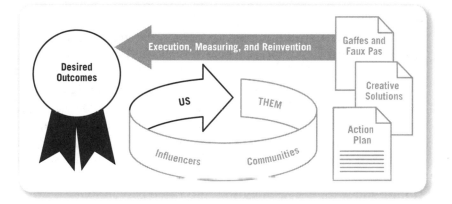

——— BRAND PERSONALITY ———

In Kafka's *Metamorphosis*, a man wakes up one morning and discovers that he has become a bug. What if your brand woke up one morning and discovered it had become a human? And let's say the human came to your house and knocked on the door. Who would you meet? What kind of person does your brand look like? Would you be inclined to invite it in for coffee?

It's been suggested that people project personalities or *personas* onto brands. Wanting to test that notion ourselves here at DragonSearch, we created boards of photos of different people and took them out into the streets of our little town. We asked people, "If such-and-such brand came to life, who would the brand most look like?"

71

The results were surprisingly consistent. Starbucks was most frequently compared to a soccer mom. Google was a hip, young Asian guy. And BP was a grumpy, middle-aged businessman (not a surprise, given that our impromptu survey took place in the months after the BP oil spill). We later discovered that similar studies were conducted by J. Walter Thompson Advertising Agency in the early 1960s with results that reinforced the idea that people project personalities onto brands.

> The organization's voice is just one of many consistently touching on subjects of core interest to its identity and activities.
>
> —**Admiral Gary Roughead,** Chief of Naval Operations, US Navy

Brand Traits

In the late 1990s, social psychologist and marketer Jennifer Aaker studied hundreds of personality traits often associated with brands. Psychologists often refer to a "Big Five" list of personality traits. Aaker wanted to see if the personality traits that people ascribe to brands could be similarly classified. In her robust study, the five brands traits she identified included sincerity, excitement, competence, sophistication, and ruggedness (Table 5.1). Each of those traits has multiple facets, which in turn encompass several character traits. Aaker then used those attributes as a means for scaling and testing how brands fit into those perceptions.

TABLE 5.1 Brand Personality Traits

PERSONALITY TRAIT	FACETS	ATTRIBUTES
Sincerity	Down-to-earth	Down-to-earth
		Family-oriented
		Small-town
	Honest	Honest
		Sincere
		Real
	Wholesome	Wholesome
		Original
	Cheerful	Cheerful
		Sentimental
		Friendly

PERSONALITY TRAIT	FACETS	ATTRIBUTES
Excitement	Daring	Daring
		Trendy
		Exciting
	Spirited	Spirited
		Cool
		Young
	Imaginative	Imaginative
		Unique
	Up-to-date	Up-to-date
		Independent
		Contemporary
Competence	Reliable	Reliable
		Hard working
		Secure
	Intelligent	Intelligent
		Technical
		Corporate
	Successful	Successful
		Leader
		Confident
Sophistication	Upper class	Upper class
		Glamorous
		Good looking
	Charming	Charming
		Feminine
		Smooth
Ruggedness	Outdoorsy	Outdoorsy
		Masculine
		Western
	Tough	Tough
		Rugged

Marketing is both a practical endeavor and an area of academic study, so it isn't surprising that there is quibbling about the taxonomy of personality attributes, but the important takeaway for marketers is that people do indeed project personalities onto brands—and it is within our power to help shape those mental images. Instead of only creating persona boards for your customers, create one for your brand. As a brand steward, you have to ask yourself: If my brand came to life, who would it be? Who would I *like* it to be?

By doing so, you'll get a quick mental picture to test any language or conversation against. At my own company, we envisioned the DragonSearch brand as Harrison Ford in the Indiana Jones movies—professorial on one hand, but not unwilling to pull out a bullwhip and fight off bad guys if necessary.

Freud postulated the idea of projection—we project onto others what we're not allowed to feel or are ashamed to feel. Jung took it further with his concept of archetypes. There is a lot of talk about *aspirational* attributes: what people *want* to be or how they want to be perceived. My hunch is that the complex sensory machines that are humans need to project, simplify, and think in terms of archetypes in order to make sense of the complexities of modern life. The perception of a brand's personality is built up from every single touchpoint that the consumer (or audience) has with the brand. The more consistently you communicate your desired attributes, the more likely consumers are to form a strong sense of your brand's personality.

How We Relate to Brands

People feel enthusiasm for brands at all different levels. If you manufacture spot remover that is used in the dry cleaning industry, you aren't going to have the same type of relationship with the general public that a sportswear manufacturer might. The challenge is to find a place in the hearts and minds of the people who do matter to your brand.

Brands can be grouped into three buckets based on how we relate to them:

1. The brand that we take for granted. We don't swoon when we see the logo, but we trust it. If it were a person, we'd say hello and perhaps go for a beer at the local bar. I go to my local grocery store every week and like it well enough. But if a competitor opened up down the street, I'd have no hesitation in trying it out.

2. The brand that we really, really like. We would like to have dinner with this brand, even go on a date. I feel this way

about certain consumer goods I purchase. I'll go out of my way to buy them.

3. The brand that we'd bring home to meet our parents. We want to marry this brand. Harley-Davidson, Apple, and even Crayola Crayons. People get tattoos of these brands' logos inked onto their bodies.

Depending on the industry you're in, it may not be feasible to move into the third bucket, but if you're in the first, you want to be moving toward the second.

BRAND VOICE

Brands can talk now. Perhaps they did before, a little, but nowhere near the extent they can now. A brand can have a Facebook page, a Twitter profile, a Google Plus page, and any number of the other social media platform profiles. The brand can be host to communities and can itself be heard in a myriad of other communities.

Values, Vision, and Passion

The brand personality is the basis for the brand voice—that aggregate of tone, intention, and language that is uttered wherever the brand is heard, even in text. The development of voice is another reason that an organization's vision, values, and passion need to be clearly articulated. These are the very elements that guide that voice's creation.

Plural or Individual Voice

This is where an interesting conundrum arises for brand marketers: one line of branding thought is that we should speak for the brand in third person, as in, "Acme Soda is delighted to be sponsoring Pleasantville's tenth anniversary fund-raiser." Others maintain that people are not interested in interacting with a corporate entity and that people like to deal with other people. Brand communicators are sometimes at odds about this. @Ford, the official Twitter account for the Ford Motor Company, uses the first-person plural "we" and "our." @Pepsi, this morning, said, "Who loves sleeping in, we do! We do!"

When do social media voices speak for the collective "we" as opposed to speaking for an individual? In being social on behalf of a brand, we're going to come across in a more genuine light, with more sincerity, if we speak as individuals. This challenge of choosing between a plural voice and individual voices is going to be approached differently by different types of organizations. If yours is a service-centered organization, individual voices might be more important than they would be in a product-based organization. Also, the decision will depend on how well you're able to activate social media across the organization or the brand.

Culture

As Todd Wilms of SAP put it, "I think the biggest thing for us—and we've talked a lot about this with other customers and companies, and again as we've been out on the road evangelizing—it's about knowing the culture of your company. You know the culture of SAP and the culture of Dell and the culture of Pepsi and the culture of Puma, they are all different cultures, they are all different backgrounds, they are coming at the markets from a different way, they have different business problems. To do a one-size-fits-all social media strategy for them I think is disingenuous. So what works for SAP might not work for Dell, what works for Dell might not work for Puma. What we really had to come back to—'What is the corporate culture of SAP?' 'What does SAP want to accomplish?' 'How does it view social media?' 'Is it about crowdsourcing and new product ideas?' 'Is it about customer service and engaging people through a variety of different channels instead of phone and e-mail forms?' 'Is it about marketing and marketing messaging?' 'Is it about community and community engagement?' 'What's our core culture?' So we always had to bring it back to [core culture], and this is what we advise to a lot of other brands and other companies, . . . stick to your core culture. If your culture is 'hey, we're going to market and that's how we do social media,' then don't try pushing crowdsourcing and product ideas in that organization because you're going upstream against the culture."

How Smart Is Your Brand?

Throughout the twentieth century, academics worked to devise a method of analyzing text and applying to it a system of levels. In the 1970s, the US Navy merged a couple of different systems and, in the process, applied grade levels. That system, the Flesch-Kincaid Grade Level Formula, is often used today to assess the reading level of any given text. While I don't recommend running every blog post through an online tester, doing so every now and then can spark good conversation about how advanced your writing is and how advanced it *should* be.

Smartness isn't just about vocabulary but about sentence length and sentence structure as well as the underlying topics. If your brand is aimed at average consumers, you don't want to sound like a consultant from the Rand Corporation.

How Friendly Is Your Brand?

There's an old salesman's trick of having a mirror close to your phone so that when you're on a call, you'll remember to smile while you're talking. The belief is that your smile is communicated subtly in the way you speak. While not every situation calls for friendliness, the majority of human interactions go more smoothly when people are smiling and being friendly. How friendly should your brand be? In developing your brand's personal attributes, consider this question and then test your communications against where you wish to be. Sometimes the difference between a piece of friendly communication and a cold-fish handshake is subtle.

Note how in this Facebook post, Mini Cooper is friendly without being an over-the-top cheerleader: "This is your official warning: you have 6 days left to secure your Co-Pilot seat in the MINI Coupé headed to ALL THE WRONG PLACES. This time, that place is South Africa. Coming with? Apply now!" Chevrolet has a post that is similar in content but slightly different: "Here's your last chance to vote for the Best Chevy of All Time. The '69 Camaro leads the '70 Chevelle SS by 1,333 votes. Which one do you think should wear the crown? Vote now."

Perhaps Mini Cooper is striving to be a little more familiar with that "coming with"? This isn't to say the Chevrolet social media team is doing anything wrong here. In fact, Chevrolet also has a lot of posts up about safety—and it's true, if you want to be regarded highly in safety, you might choose to play down the party tone. In working with your own brand, if you want to be higher on the conviviality scale, keep an eye on just how friendly you really are.

Aligning the brand with a cause (or *cause marketing*, as it's being referred to) is an opportunity to be human and friendly and to show a caring side. Some of the most successful social media campaigns to date have been cause-marketing based. They're successful because the sponsoring organization is explicitly *not* being promotional but rather is aligning with an underlying passion point.

Your voice also needs to work across different regions of the world. If yours is a global company, you need to develop guidelines around the voice specific to different regions as well as an understanding of where you're going to focus.

Speaking Through Social Media

There may be no place more important to the development of your brand voice than social media. Certainly, there are brands that lend themselves to being self-promotional—the brand's audience loves the brand for what it is. In our work for a national discount department store, followers and fans wanted to be privy to early information about sales, discounts, and new products.

Other brands, though, don't lend themselves to that sort of customer loyalty, and they need to find the deeper passion points for people to connect with.

Every decent book on marketing, business, and strategy talks about differentiation. What better way is there to differentiate your brand than by letting it come to life and be a voice for the issues that matter to your customers?

Stephanie Schwab of *Social Media Explorer* suggests that there are four components to a brand voice:

1. Character/persona
2. Tone
3. Language
4. Purpose[1]

Kitty Sheehan, at Frontier Natural Products, told this story: "One day, one of our marketing managers said, 'I like the voice of Dick Cavett. Let's have our voice sound like Dick Cavett.' He was kidding in a way, but we all kind of started talking about that. I brought in some of Dick Cavett's writing, we read it, and we laughed. It was funny, and smart. And I keep that in the back of my mind, 'what would Dick Cavett say?'"

There are different schools of thought when it comes to brand voice. The first maintains that the brand's voice should be paramount. It's not a "we," or "we at Brand X," but "Brand X." And thus the individual's voice is subjugated to the brand's voice.

This idea is discussed by Shiv Singh in his book *Social Media Marketing for Dummies*. Singh suggests that instead of just brand voice, organizations also need to create guidelines for what he calls the social influence marketing (SIM) voice. The SIM voice comprises multiple, authentic individual voices and may sometimes deviate from the brand voice. The SIM voice isn't an alternative to the brand voice; it's what the brand voice needs to become: pluralistic.

Old-school marketing would say, "Define your brand voice, and everyone will speak with that voice." But as the idea of SIM suggests, that is neither feasible nor realistic. There is simply too much to be gained from allowing individuals to sing from the mountaintops, being themselves and being a part of the larger organization. On the other hand, as I mentioned earlier, the more consistently a brand's personality is communicated, the more real it becomes. This paradox is real, and it has to be navigated.

To what extent individual voices can be a prominent part of your social media will depend on your organization. You may have your main corporate or brand voices, which play a certain role, while individuals participate in their own way. Done well, the brand can enhance what the individuals are doing, and the individuals can enhance what the brand voice is saying. SAP and Intel are good examples of brands that have struck a nice balance between brand voice and individual voices, and while these are large, global companies, there isn't any reason why the same kind of balance can't be achieved in a small organization as well.

Stephanie Weingart of BlueGlass Interactive suggests that a voice that works on one platform might not work on another. Platforms often comprise completely different audiences, and it just wouldn't make sense to address one group of people the same as you'd address another.

BRAND VOICES IN SOCIAL MEDIA

As a friend of mine, a veteran of the old Madison Avenue public relations firms, reminds me, a brand is a mental construct. As such, it can be eroded by anything that deviates from its essence. There is a series of voices that we've identified as being particularly strong in social media. You can adopt any one voice or create a mixture of different voices.

Maven Voice

The word *maven* comes from the Yiddish word meaning "expert," but the word possesses certain connotations. Someone can be an expert, but if she keeps all of her knowledge to herself, you wouldn't call that person a maven. A maven shares. Perhaps that's because the word was popularized in the 1960s in radio commercials for herring featuring a character aptly named the Herring Maven. William Safire, who penned a popular column, referred to himself as a language maven. Malcolm Gladwell cited the "maven" as one of the personality types needed to help a concept go viral. Being a maven is different from simply being knowledgeable or professorial. Mavens know their stuff, and they're willing to share.

On the Bobbi Brown Cosmetics social accounts, Ms. Brown, or someone speaking for her, constantly provides good advice on using makeup. They aren't saying, oh, use *this* lipstick, and *this* skin toner (although they do sometimes refer to particular products)—but instead, they provide more general advice like, "For a modern take on a matte lip, create a soft, stained finish by applying lip color to your bottom lip only and pressing your lips together."

Using the maven voice in social media is powerful because, on one hand, your voice becomes a source of influence, being credible and knowledgeable. Plus you're being friendly and generous, which invokes the power of reciprocity in influence. You're not alienating your audience with anything that might have a whiff of self-promotion. If I sense you're trying to sell me something, I have to be on my guard, whereas if I feel you're just being a great source of information, I can let my guard down. I might even fall in love with your brand.

Voice of Passion

One of the most interesting voices to emerge in new media is the voice of passion. This is the voice of someone who takes on a topic with enthusiasm and owns it. Instead of talking about whatever it is they sell, passionate voices talk about the something that stands behind the brand. You see this in Coca-Cola's social media campaign, where the brand chooses three people, gives them travel expenses and video cameras, and asks them to document how people express happiness around the world.

It's more important than ever for brand managers to identify the passion points behind their brand. A perfect example is Nike on its Facebook page: not one post is self-promotional. Instead, each and every post speaks to the passion behind the company.

One might argue that Nike has an incredible marketing budget, so it can afford to talk from its passion points; a company that makes dish soap, on the other hand, would have to be more overtly promotional. That argument just doesn't hold. Martha Stewart's magazine and television show, for example, proved that people could be very passionate about homemaking, which one might consider just as mundane as soap.

Voice of Advocacy

The voice of advocacy is similar to the voice of passion. It speaks on someone's behalf. Aflac, for example, speaks on behalf of a cause, the treatment of cancer in children.

Voice of Community Love

The voice of community love can be an expression of love for a physical or a virtual community. Glenwood Management is a real estate management company in Manhattan. Instead of simply using social media to promote its properties, as many real estate companies do, the company celebrates the communities where its properties are located.

Customer Focus Voice

What would any marketer not give to get feedback like this?

"If I could marry a company, it would be Zappos," one visitor posted to the Zappos Facebook page. Zappos, of course, is famous for its customer care focus. This focus extends to the company's Facebook page. Zappos rarely makes posts of its own; primarily, the company responds to customer comments.

Promotional Voice

The promotional voice constantly brings attention back to the products or services of the company. Promotion isn't just advertising; it's any activity that helps to bring the brand into greater awareness with the audience. Contests and advertising both are forms of promotion.

If a brand has a strong community of loyal customers, the promotional voice can be effective. For instance, customers of Audi and Burberry *want* to bring exposure to the products. But if your brand doesn't have that kind of customer loyalty, the promotional voice can be the least favorable to use in social media. People don't care about your making money or not, and attempts to sell in social media can be met with fierce opposition. In the absence of strong customer loyalty, you're better off finding the passion behind the brand and working from that position.

You may put a great deal of effort into developing your place in a community, carefully crafting your brand voice. One day, your manager calls you in and says that something has to be done about sales numbers. For a moment, you're tempted to go to your community and make them a great offer. Don't do it. If the voice you've cultivated doesn't include a salesperson, then the mental construct that is your brand will crumble. There will be cognitive dissonance.

Mixing Voice Types

Ultimately, your brand's voice is most likely to comprise a combination of voices. When you are truly working from a point of passion, you are part of a community, and you are an advocate. And sometimes, in order to provide the most value to your community, it's even necessary to be a little self-promotional. Finding the right mix for your brand is the key. I would encourage you to think twice about pushing the promotional voice too much. When executives are demanding immediate upticks in sales, remind them that effective social media marketing involves creating long-term brand equity.

OTHER WAYS TO HUMANIZE THE BRAND

In 1886, the US Supreme Court decided on the case of *County of Santa Clara v. the Southern Pacific Railroad*, granting corporations status as individuals, and while this has long been the case in the eyes of the law, everyone still knows the difference. As marketers, though, we also know that the more individualized a brand is, the more likely consumers are to spend with that brand. It's taken over 120 years, but with social media, we're enabling the brand to become a little more like the court said.

Anything we can do to help the brand seem more individual, the better. In tweeting, or other places where members of the team can post, encourage behavior that emphasizes their individuality.

Depending on the brand and the makeup of the social media team, you'll need to decide whether to maintain the voice of the brand as one single voice, leaving out the individuality of people *in* the brand, or allowing the individual voices to come forward.

Pepsi's Twitter profile is clearly maintained by a five-person social media team, with their names mentioned on the profile page. On some profiles, such as McGraw-Hill's, photos of individuals are included, which helps to reinforce the fact that there are real people behind the profile.

STAYING ON VOICE

If you run through all of the brand social media profiles you can think of, you're likely to find that most of them struggle to stay on voice and on message. Social media marketing teams change personnel; people get busy with various other tasks. For these and other reasons, it's important to review your account periodically to make sure you're maintaining voice.

Even one of my personal favorites, Nike, has been slipping into a more self-promotional voice lately, although perhaps by design.

✓ CHECKLIST

1. Audit the existing brand voice and how it is used in social media and other communications.

   ☐ Notice your brand voice—how is it being used? Is it promotional? maven? passion-based?

   ☐ Do you have a brand-voice document?

   ☐ Is everyone on the social media team aware of what the voice should be?

   ☐ Is there training on the voice?

2. Your brand voice document should include the following:

   ☐ Useful vocabulary—particularly words that might frequently be used in your industry. Also, create a list of words that shouldn't be used.

   ☐ Examples in different social media—show what your social media postings should look like. As you go along, add "best of" to the collection.

   ☐ Writing guidelines—this is something that can grow with time. Consider

   ○ Names, nicknames

   ○ Personality

   ○ Core values

   ○ Passion

   ○ Slogan or catch phrase

   ○ Visual style

   ○ Verbal style

3. Institute a monthly brand voice review.

CHAPTER 6

FINDING THE FRINGE
IDENTIFYING CUSTOMER MICROSEGMENTS

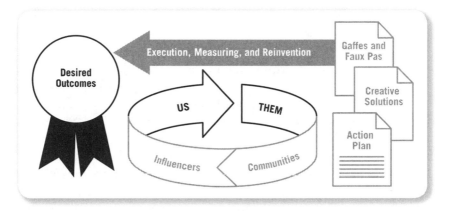

MARKET SEGMENTATION

If you drive north of New York City for about 90 miles, you'll come to a bucolic mountainous region called the Catskills. Several years ago, before the social media era, I was part of a multiagency team marketing a new luxury resort in that region. As the property was a fairly upscale vacation getaway, we were seeking potential customers who could afford to pay a few extra dollars to escape the vagaries of city life and enjoy a few days of being pampered. In consideration of the fact that we were appealing to affluent consumers in the New York City area, that was a fairly simple task. There wasn't a whole lot more to our target demographics—if they were old enough to drive and could afford a couple of nights lodging and a spa treatment, we wanted them. Media kits were ordered from a few dozen magazines, demographic tables sorted through, and CPM (cost per mille) figures scratched out on paper.

We spread the costs out over the year, targeting those times when occupancy was lowest, and *presto!* a media spending plan was born.

Of course, if we had special events such as an antique car show, we could target antique car fanatics, or if we had a show of antique maps, we could target cartography aficionados. And over time, once reservation tracking codes were used, we could even see that some of the fashion magazines were more effective than other publications. But all in all, we were aiming a short-barreled shotgun at the side of a barn; our tools were scattershot and our target was wide.

Up until the digital era, mass advertising was relatively unspecific. In newspapers, advertisements could be run alongside regular columns or in particular sections; in broadcast media, your commercial could air during a certain radio or television program. But in all cases, the demographics of the audiences being targeted were fairly broad. Consider the world of people out there, those multitudes who, if they knew, would love to engage your brand. Or, if yours is a B2B company, consider that small handful of people who really matter in your industry. One marketing manager at an animal pharmaceutical company told me that there were about five people in the world who really mattered to her business! Very few businesses have such a minuscule niche, but what if your own market could be subdivided into countless microaudiences?

In traditional media, there has always been a practical limit to the size of the segment that can be targeted. In twentieth-century marketing, the one exception was direct mail, wherein the marketer could focus on more specific demographics given a sufficiently granular database. We could, for instance, send to librarians and firefighters in Philadelphia an invitation to a resort in the Poconos. But as the Internet has become an established part of most Americans' lifestyle, the limitations in targeting smaller subsets of consumers have been greatly reduced, particularly in projects wherein we want to reach out to and engage individual influencers. And unlike those Publishers Clearinghouse mailers that mentioned their addressees by name and town, our audience is able to communicate back with us.

I've used the word *audience* in speaking of hypersegmentation and microaudiences, but really, the word fails us here. It implies that we are playing our tune and they are listening. The word *customers* is better, but even then, in social media, we might very well find great value in engaging with people who may not even be our customers. The other terms—*constituents*, *segments*, *targets*—all fall short as well.

HOW WE SEE SEGMENTS, NICHES, AND AUDIENCES

Market segmentation is a major task in marketing, if not an out-and-out subdiscipline. The concept of segmentation gained popularity in the 1960s as a means to offer the same products to different segments at different prices; it has also become an integral step in positioning. But even before there was a term for it, marketers used demographics to identify where they should place their advertising dollars and to guide their messages. The study of demographics covered stages in the family life cycle, gender, age, income, ethnicity, interests, and other attributes. Of course, as media became "mass," geographic or environmental segmentation followed. Radio, television, and newspapers were naturally divided into geographic markets. Billboards and other signage were bound by physical placement, and, of course, we could assume quite a bit about consumers' buying habits based on where they lived. Over time, behavioral and psychographic approaches were added.

In 1936, industry analyst Arthur C. Nielsen heard that a couple of MIT professors had invented the Audimeter, which could record when a radio was turned on and to what station it was tuned. Nielsen acquired the rights to the device, and by 1942, it had started the Nielsen Radio Index, which by 1950 was extended with the Nielsen Television Index. Up until that point, a lot of the information about media consumption habits came from labor-intensive door-to-door surveys. Nielsen's large-scale data collection allowed marketers to begin to sort consumption choices with demographic data.

After World War II, there was a marked increase in the study of clinical psychology, and with the 1957 launch of the Soviet satellite *Sputnik*, our national competitiveness spurred on a huge increase in funding of behavioral science. By the late 1960s, the new thinking was making its way to the world of marketing. Marketers became enamored of using the methodologies and discoveries of psychological and motivation research. This new approach, with the lens on values, attitudes, personality, hobbies, politics, interests, and lifestyles, was dubbed *psychograph-ics*. Advertisers had always shown psychological insight into their audiences, often quite astutely, but this new trend meant that businesses could now segment their markets based on psychologi-cal factors.

In earlier times, before the widespread use of television, geo-graphical markets tended toward more homogeneity. Today, people across the country are more likely to share certain mind-sets. For instance, in today's youth market, you'll find hip-hop fans not in one particular area but just about anywhere, be it Boise or Princeton. As Steve Route argues in his book *The Tanning of America*, there is a greater complexity of mindset that spans demographics.

When Wieden + Kennedy brought the Old Spice video cam-paign to 4chan, the irreverent and often obscene message board, they did so with a respectful understanding of the psycho-graphic makeup of that space. While the demographics of 4chan are primarily males 18 to 34 years old, users also have a keen interest in Japanese culture, manga, anime, and risqué content. Understanding the psychographic was critical in the viral spread of the irreverent humor of Isaiah Mustafa (the actor in the Old Spice videos). It's also important in such an environment to be open and unguarded, even allowing for a certain messiness in your work. A too tightly controlled corporate message wouldn't be well received.

In September 2011, Ragú distributed a video that asked, "What is dinnertime like when Dad cooks?" poking fun at dads in the kitchen. They then promoted it to "daddy bloggers" using Twitter. A savvy user of Twitter could see that Ragú was send-ing the same tweet to many other users as well. Both the video's message and the way it was distributed were antithetical to the ethos of that audience. The campaign demonstrated a clear lack of understanding of that group's psychographic profile. As marketer and author C. C. Chapman wrote, "Ragú, you failed. You tried to be clever and you blew it. Whoever your agency is that told you this was a good idea should be fired because they are doing things for you that snake oil salespeople are selling companies on every day and you've written the check for it. You should have known better. They should have served you better." With a slow follow-up, Ragú further antagonized the savvy bloggers it was trying to court.

Behavioral Segmentation

The age of Google has ushered in an entirely new model of advertising and a new capability to see how our audiences are behaving. We can document how often people return to a site, if they share with friends, if they even have friends, if they "like" something, and more. In addition to search behaviors, other aspects of behavioral segmentation include how loyal customers are to a brand, their readiness to purchase, price sensitivity, benefits sought, and other attributes.

Behavioral segmentation is closely related to psychographic segmentation. In the latter, we look more at attributes pertaining to personality, values, and lifestyles. When we talk about Generation Y, or Millennials, we're not just referring to people born in the 1980s and 1990s but to people who embody characteristics of that group, such as familiarity with the Internet. While psychographics can also help us understand some enormous dimensions of what otherwise might be wide-ranging groups, strictly speaking, it can be fairly challenging to suss out robust profiles.

Online Ethnography

Scott Briggs of Alterian described an interesting example in profiling mothers: historically a broad demographic group, mothers may play the role of confidante, nurse, friend, activist, wife, cleaner, teacher, cook, advisor, family archivist, employer, financial manager, and event planner. Alterian employs what it refers to as *virtual ethnography*, and what Robert Kozinets has termed *netnography*. Ethnography is that part of sociology or anthropology that entails the gathering of data and observations. Historically, ethnography and anthropological fieldwork in general have been subject to criticism: it's difficult for outsiders to enter a culture and to observe without affecting the culture themselves. In online ethnography, however, there is much more opportunity to gather data without the danger of creating an observer effect.

One of the tenets of social media is that brands should listen. In online ethnography, close listening can help brands and marketers identify the various psychographic or behavioral aspects of people within particular communities. For instance, in one Twitter community, I observed that users like to spend a little time on social chatter before talking about more serious issues, and that social chatter tended to be about coffee or alcohol. I now understand that when I have important information to share with that community, it might serve me well not to dispense with the niceties.

Personas

In the 1920s, advertising agencies like J. Walter Thompson endeavored to create better communications with audiences. They invited people from the tabloid and movie industries, even sociologists, to visit their office and speak to the staff. While they did tabulate brand purchases, media coverage, and indexed media buying, their understanding of their audience was still fairly generic. In fact, advertisers of that era often posited the ideal customer, which, in turn, became the aspirational lifestyle of the real customers. Advertising executives themselves tended to move further and further away from the *hoi polloi*. In an early study of personas, the Ruthrauff and Ryan agency set up a display in its reception room of two composite photographs of crowds at sporting events, allowing copywriters to consider the differences between them.

In the 1980s, software developer Alan Cooper interviewed a potential user of a piece of software he was writing. During long walks across a golf course, he would play out imaginary conversations with that person and "found that this play-acting technique was remarkably effective for cutting through complex design questions of functionality and interaction, allowing me to clearly see what was necessary and unnecessary and, more importantly, to differentiate between what was used frequently and what was needed only infrequently." Later, as a consultant, he formalized the process of imagining individuals and the documentation of that information in order to more easily communicate software requirements. In 1998, his book *The Inmates Are Running the Asylum* established the creation of personas as a standard software development practice.[1]

One of the difficulties of traditional marketing was that a business had to narrowly define its audience and even its own voice. Social media is allowing a much greater fragmentation of audiences and even voices. Using personas is one way to understand our audiences better.

INTRODUCTION TO MICROSEGMENTATION

For social media, we want to take the concept of segmentation to its extreme, to what's been called *hypergranular*, and arrive at *microsegmentation*. We want to make use of all types of segmentation—demographic, psychographic, environmental, and behavioral—in order to imagine and then discover relevant individuals and communities. Depending on what our organization is all about, we'll make use of some of these segments and discard others. The important thing is that segmentation is a tool.

At DragonSearch, we use a brainstorming technique based on the central theme question: "Who would care about this product, or who should care about this organization?" In work for a nonprofit that helped to raise funds for people in the music industry, our own social media team was at first stumped by the question; it seemed that everyone cares about music. As we drilled in, though, we realized the question we really needed to answer was: "Who cares about musicians?" That led us to a world of subsegments such as instrument makers, instrument repairers, music schools, music teachers, and music publishers.

By using the brainstorming technique first, we can get unexpected ideas and capitalize on different knowledge bases within a group. For instance, for the music nonprofit mentioned above, one of our team is an experienced musician and recording engineer himself; thus he was aware of the fact that there are special groups for recording engineers.

Drilling in like this, we're considering how those people live, think, and spend their leisure time. Their attention is ultimately spent on the things that interest them. These aren't segments in the classic marketing sense at all, but *microsegments*. This is what some people have called *hypersegmentation*.

Another example was a client of ours that manufactured crystal for the luxury market. Steuben covered a wide terrain, a few examples being crystal baseball bats, ice fishing, and pandas. Steuben offered hundreds of different animal figures in its signature optical crystal. In reaching out through social media, it was able to divide animal lovers into several groups: domestic, wildlife, and farm. In domestic, the breakdown went further, into cats, dogs, birds, and fish. In dogs, of course, there are people who love particular breeds as well as aficionados of obedience training, show dogs, and pets. Lovers of particular breeds could be further broken down into smaller groups, like the Airedale Terrier Club of Greater Atlanta.

In the creation of a long list of these small groups, we're then able to discover where those groups are online, and who influences them. This is the promise of *microsegmentation*.

By brainstorming a world of microsegments, the social media team is able to create an encyclopedia of opportunities for connecting with potential customers on a highly customized basis. Social media has empowered marketers to connect with very small interest and affinity groups at a new level.

There are many considerations in looking at potential groups to interact with in social media. First of all, it's not enough to interact only with customers and potential customers. All around them are other people exerting influence of some sort or another. I've often seen children at the grocery story begging their mothers to buy something. They aren't the buyers, but they are the influencers. When creating your microsegmentation, consider who is *influencing* your customers.

Other tools that can be used in addition to brainstorming include audience or customer segments that parallel your main audience, nested segmentation, and keyword research. One of the benefits of hypersegmentation is that we are working with small groups—we can iterate quickly through groups to see where we fit and to see if we get a response. If we don't, we move on to the next one, quickly.

Microaudience Brainstorming

Start with a central question: who should care about what we do, or what we sell, or who we are? Sometimes, this simple question brings forth a geyser of useful concepts; other times, you get only tumbleweeds and crickets. If the latter, you can work through a thinking tree like this:

- ► Who benefits from this?
- ► How do they benefit? Who will suffer if this isn't successful?

We went through this process for a book I wrote, a basic primer on online marketing for entrepreneurs and small business people. When starting out, we hit the wall when we asked, "Who would benefit from this book?" The answer ("All small business people and entrepreneurs") was too general. But as we started to think about the world of those people, we started remembering all of the other people who are committed to helping small businesses and entrepreneurs, such as business coaches at SCORE, the Small Business Administration, Chambers of Commerce, teachers of business at colleges and high schools, website hosting companies, companies that sell online advertising, and more.

Another question to ask is, "What is our passion point, and who shares that passion?" You can even place that question in the middle of the brainstorming board. In order to tease out ideas, it can be helpful to have a lot of people in the room, people who know the brand or business from different angles.

Ultimately, the brainstorming session can be summarized in a bulleted list. This list should be maintained as a living document. As you identify new subsegments or groups, add them. Once you've identified a large variety of subsegments, you can start to research where those people inhabit the social space. That research represents an ongoing activity in which you are constantly identifying new microaudiences. Also, as you identify the communities where those audiences participate, you'll be led to even more microaudiences and their influencers. The whole exercise constantly provides a richer and richer context for the marketer.

All of the segmenting approaches mentioned above are filters that are available to us in microaudience brainstorming. If the brainstorming gets stuck, go to the segmentation checklist at the end of the chapter, applying the approaches to the segments that you have identified, and see if any others emerge.

Over time, add attributes to these segments, particularly as you're able to identify subgroups based on previously unimagined attributes. For instance, we went down this path:

Who cares about musicians? People at music schools. People at Berkeley. People at Berkeley who are interested in world music. People at Berkeley who are interested in zydeco dancing. In other words, it went from central theme, to education (broad), to education (specific), to cultural taste (broad), to cultural taste (specific). Investigation of those microaudiences led to yet more microaudiences!

Parallel Audiences

Mari Luangrath started her cupcake company Foiled in 2009. In the break between when she acquired her license and when Foiled was able to begin production, Mari jumped onto Twitter and started to connect with people in her area who shared an interest in things like pop culture, weather, chocolate, travel, music, and, most pointedly, shoes. It turned out that if a Chicago suburbanite had an interest in certain types of not-so-cheap designer shoes, then she was also a very likely customer for Foiled Cupcakes. In all of our microaudience work, we can seek out such parallel interests. For instance, if someone were interested in caviar, he would be likely to be interested in Steuben.

In Microaudience brainstorming, pose this question for each user type that you identify: "What else do they really like?" If you have time, you can even go so far as to create a miniprofile of each type, describing such things as main interests. In segmentation work, these proxy variables can often help you identify a microsegmentation in a way that an actual attribute cannot.[2]

In the 1980s, industrial marketers developed an approach to identifying markets known as *nested segmentation*. In *How to Segment Industrial Markets* by Benson Shapiro and Thomas Bonoma, the authors propose nested segmentation criteria of demographics, operating variables, customer purchasing approaches, situational factors, and personal characteristics of buyers. The method was called *nested* because marketers would start with the larger overarching circle of demographics and drill in to central personal characteristics, a process similar to opening a Russian matryoshka doll.

In both paid search and search engine optimization (SEO), there is a tradition of performing keyword analysis as an initial and necessary step. That research tells marketers which words and phrases people in the real world are actually searching, as opposed to the words and phrases the marketer imagines people are searching. Often this analysis is performed by compiling a *seed list* comprising words and phrases the marketing team and other stakeholders believe are relevant. The analyst will often analyze competitive sites as well to determine what phrases those marketers believe are important.

The seed list is then run through one or more tools, such as Google's Keyword Tool, to expand upon that list, pulling out associated phrases. Then, finally, that larger list is edited for nonrelevant keywords and run through another tool that indicates the quantity of real searches for those phrases during a set time period.

The resulting document can help the marketer brainstorm topics that hadn't been considered, recognize interests, identify affinity groups, and search out influencers using those phrases.

— MICROSEGMENTS EXERCISE —

This is a brainstorming exercise. It can be done with the marketing team alone or can include other stakeholders, such as executives, salespeople, and customer support. As an agency, we've had great success including our client in this process.

Start with a central question, such as "Who should care about our company?" or "Who might care about this product?"

Next, find the major groups of customers or interest groups, and branch off from there, as in the example in Figure 6.1.

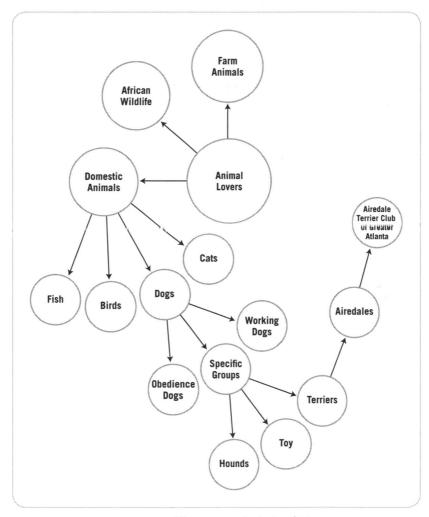

FIGURE 6.1 Microsegment brainstorming

At the conclusion of the brainstorming, photograph the board and have someone transcribe the groups into a bulleted list. The resulting document will be critical in the social media marketing process and should be a living document, frequently consulted, updated, and used for inspiration. If possible, make a large drawing, or dedicate a whiteboard to the microsegmentation brainstorming. Your microsegments become your blueprint for social media activities.

For each microsegment identified, research each group, taking note of where group members are showing up in social media and which key phrases are prominent. Within social media groups, take note of which individuals seem to be respected and have what appear to be leading roles.

CONCLUSION

Unlike traditional advertising, where you are committing to a large spend, in social media, you are doing small pieces of work. You can afford to go after a particular microaudience for a couple of days and see if you gain some traction. If not, you can move on to the next. Also, your microsegmentation can help you identify audiences that can then be targeted for more expensive and commitment-intensive campaigns.

✓ CHECKLIST

Geographic or Environmental Segmentation
- [ ] Region
- [ ] Time zone
- [ ] Climate
- [ ] International or domestic
- [ ] Urban, suburban, or rural

Demographic Segmentation
- [ ] Age
- [ ] Gender
- [ ] Ethnicity
- [ ] Education, colleges or schools attended
- [ ] Social class
- [ ] Occupation
- [ ] Family status
- [ ] Income
- [ ] How a person relates to a company or organization
  - ○ Role in organization
  - ○ Time in organization
  - ○ Department
  - ○ Employee status

Psychographic Segmentation
- [ ] Values
- [ ] Attitudes
- [ ] Beliefs
- [ ] Lifestyle

Behavioral Segmentation
- [ ] Behavioral patterns
- [ ] Price sensitivity
- [ ] Brand loyalty
- [ ] Benefits sought
- [ ] How information is sought
- [ ] Buying behaviors

CHAPTER 7

BIRDS OF A FEATHER
BELONGING TO A COMMUNITY

THE ESSENCE OF A COMMUNITY

Imagine telling the great nineteenth-century department store magnate John Wanamaker that in addition to running a successful business, negotiating the needs of thousands of employees, and still turning a profit, he should create and participate in communities that are aligned to the interests of his business. And imagine telling him that if he did so, his stores would benefit because stockholders, the public, and employees would all hold the business in greater esteem and have a stronger desire to shop at Wanamaker's.

Not that you'd need to tell Wanamaker. Interestingly, he was a huge proponent of community activism, not only by being a leader in the YMCA and church but also by hosting educational and development programs in the basement of his department store. The phrase *corporate welfare* has come to refer to how society supports corporations, but it was originally coined to refer to the programs that large companies put into place to support their employees and surrounding communities. The values Wanamaker espoused in his nonbusiness communities were the very values that he expected his employees to uphold, values that shaped a pioneering concept of customer satisfaction. When his body was laid to rest, the entire city of Philadelphia closed for business, and tens of thousands of citizens turned out to bid him good-bye.

In 2010, after nearly five million barrels of oil flowed into the Gulf of Mexico, imagine how differently events might have unfolded had BP been a central member of the Gulf of Mexico ecology community. No doubt, it would have influenced the community's perception of the oil giant and might have had an impact on the corporation's culture even before the tragedy.

Belonging to a community doesn't simply mean that you are influencing the community but that the community is likewise influencing your organization. The potential benefits flow both ways. And by identifying your relevant communities and becoming fully involved, you make it much more difficult for competitors to obtain any hegemony. Not that a community can't contain more than one competing brand. More than one oil company could certainly be involved in a regional ecology community. The community of bourbon aficionados certainly has room for Maker's Mark as well as Knob Creek.

> All the Birds in the Air on the Earth, and the Waters, have a mutual Correspondence, Rendezvous, and Understanding with those of the same Feather; and nothing but destruction can separate them. They may be scatter'd, or dispersed for a Time into different Corners and Quarters of the Country; but they will still be upon the Wing to find out their stragglers, and flock together again.
>
> —**Oswald Dykes,** in *English Proverbs with Moral Reflexions*, 1713

Traditionally, *community* implied a physical grouping of people. With the maturation of transportation and communications, the term has become more fluid. Today, a community can exist in many different places online: bulletin boards, blogs, and even on microblogs. We are brought close not by proximity but by what we value.

After working through the audience microsegmentation covered in the previous chapter, you should find out where those audiences (customers, consumers, constituents, etc.) aggregate online. It's inevitable that you discover existing groups, cliques, and communities, or "birds of a feather." A community can be formed on a discussion board, from commenters on a blog, on Twitter, and on a Facebook group page. The individuals who contribute to a particular Wikipedia page could even constitute a community. In the online world, communities can form and adjourn quickly. This happens offline as well. People can start an instant community at a bus stop, in line at the grocery store, or even riding an elevator.

FINDING COMMUNITIES

After you've done the audience microsegmentation exercise, you'll end up with an extensive spreadsheet listing each of those microsegments. Using search engines, you can then drill down on each of those subsegments to determine if they're already on the web and, if so, where.

For instance, as mentioned in the last chapter, we did an exercise at DragonSearch for a nonprofit dedicated to helping people in the music industry. At first, the brainstorming team was baffled by the question, "Who cares about music?" The answer was simply too broad: everyone. But when the question was reframed as, "Who should care about musicians?" a lot of great ideas surfaced. In just one branch of the brainstorming tree, we began with "People in music education." Of all the ideas for music schools that were added to the whiteboard, one was the Berkeley School of Music. From there, we came up with people interested in world music at Berkeley. Finally, a search for " 'world music' + Berkeley" returned results that included the Berkeley World Music Festival and Ashkenaz Music & Dance Community Center.

Besides dozens of blogs mentioning these events and venues, many band pages are listed, along with radio stations. Right off the bat, the Berkeley World Music Festival page shows that it has a Facebook page and Twitter.

Drilling in on some of those pages reveals even more subsegments. For instance, on the Ashkenaz page, we've learned that there are Cajun/zydeco dance lessons. We could even drill down to individuals talking about Cajun music and find their communities—but since the team already has a robust dictionary of microsegments to connect with, we'll save those for later. At least on a higher level, I can start to catalog the salient communities. Some of these are clearly structured groups, like Facebook pages, while others are more ephemeral, like the people who comment on the San Francisco newspaper website.

As we go along, we make a record of the communities we find, how many participants, and any other pieces of information that jump out at the researcher.

TABLE 7.1 Music Lover Subcommunities

SITE/COMMUNITY	PARTICIPANTS	NOTES
http://twitter.com/#!/berkeleywm	24	Not particularly active
http://www.facebook.com/BerekeleyWorldMusicFestival	289	Not particularly active
http://www.facebook.com/event.php?eid=249174435104424	28+	Event August 27, 2011

As you can see from Table 7.1, these communities are of modest size, but they still offer opportunities for the social media team to make what we call *love taps*—small one-off communications. For instance, we can go to the event page listed in Table 7.1 and wish the members success with their event. Sometimes someone in that community takes note, responds, and then we have another individual to connect with. We don't try to jump into all of the communities at once but rather prioritize, based on where we think we'll have the most success. As our social media endeavors mature, we can circle back to investigate other communities in more depth.

This approach is markedly different from going to large communities that comprise thousands of individuals. Here, our approach is to find microcommunities, or small groups, and engage on the individual level.

The question will be, "How scalable is focusing on small groups and individuals?" In a world where we're accustomed to blasting messages out to hundreds of thousands or millions, it may seem strange to target only a few. If a person wakes up in the morning and starts work immediately, how many people can she interact with in a day? The difference here is that we're targeting individuals who are deeply involved with particular subjects—and in doing so, we build up a mass of communications that takes on its own life.

CREATING COMMUNITIES

For many niche products or interests, you will often find that a community doesn't exist yet, or it existed at some point and faded away. This means that you have an opportunity to create or resurrect that community and play a pivotal role.

If a community already exists, it rarely makes sense to create a similar new community. As Evan Vogel from Night Agency said, "Fish where the fish are—find a way to merge a greater message into different behaviors that people are already doing as opposed to creating new behaviors."

With over 600 million blogs, why would you create a community? What would your goals be? Temporary or permanent communities can be created around your brands or around any other attribute with which you might segment audiences or markets. Sometimes, your topics of interest are so fringe that groups dedicated to them just haven't formed. While some topics aren't central enough to anyone to hold a community together, you might uncover something that hasn't been created but is nevertheless much needed.

Many platforms on the market allow you to create custom communities using common social functionality. There's been a great deal of success with these types of communities in the health industry, where the communities have a compelling need to be closed to the public. Consider a custom closed community when privacy issues are a concern and when being closed is likely to foster a willingness among members to be social.

Community Around a Brand Passion Point

You might have one of those brands that inspires customers to tattoo your logo on their bodies. Communities form readily around such well-loved brands. It's been suggested, however, that when people tattoo the logo of Harley-Davidson, Crayola, Apple, or Walmart on their bodies, they are very likely identifying with the brand attributes as opposed to showing loyalty to the company behind the brand.[1] By focusing on brand attributes, we have the opportunity to create powerful communities, just as Nike did in using the passion of people overcoming limitations.

If your brand sells spaghetti sauce, you could develop a community around the culture of cooking and caregiving. If you sell dish soap, you can create a community around the passion of taking care of one's home. Every brand has opportunities to work from passion points. While the idea of building a community around dish soap may seem untenable, building around purpose and meaning makes sense. Even beyond your work in social media, pursuing that type of purpose can strengthen and reinvigorate the brand at many other levels as well.

Community Around a Blog

If you have identified particular influencers within your subject areas, you can refer to individuals (as appropriate) within blog posts. Then, follow up by mentioning the person on Twitter, Google Plus, or other social platforms where that person spends time and let her know that you did so. If the person comments, be sure to reply. But don't just focus on the highest level of influencers lest you appear disingenuous. Mention and call out other people who are apt to respond and get involved in the conversation.

If you participate regularly in chats and forums, you're going to encounter topics suitable for your blog posts. If you blog on such a topic, it would be totally appropriate to mention the other people who were involved in the chat, their contributions, and then to give them shout-outs after the post is live, in effect inviting them to comment on the post.

Of course, you'd want to visit those individuals' blogs and comment on their blog posts as well. In doing so, you become part of a social media blog ecosystem that in essence constitutes a community. You will start to see many of the same people in these circles and, often, a high level of participation. A good community manager can help nurture these conversations, deftly encouraging involvement across multiple platforms, and can pull in new community members.

KNOWING YOUR COMMUNITIES

Fortunate is the brand manager responsible for understanding a particular segmentation. Some companies have products or services that serve fuzzier, more elusive segments, while others are implicitly built around an existing demographic or psychographic. MTV takes on the task of understanding its audience the way Melville took on the subject of whales. MTV conducts

5 to 20 custom studies each year, hosts regular panels, and has an employee base composed mostly of Millennials.

Millennials, or Generation Y, typically thought of as those born between the mid-1980s through the mid- to late 1990s, are not simply an age demographic; they also possess a cohesive set of behaviors, norms, and attitudes. They are also notable in that they are the first generation that grew up with the Internet.

According to Britta Schell, MTV's director of digital strategic insights, MTV has come to understand that Millennials'

> level of engagement as digital natives gives them a very strong bullshit meter as they know all the ins and outs and all the tricks. They understand that their time and their eyeballs are incredibly valuable. They know that brands see social media communities as essentially a platform for the brand and recognize that they are being marketed to.
>
> It's important for brands to realize that Millennials approve if there's relevance, quality, and depth of engagement to the marketing medium or the content surrounding the marketing, as opposed to just treating it as another broadcast platform. In fact, Millennials have a very finely tuned sense and will help a brand define what is relevant and how they can participate successfully.
>
> Overall, this generation demands transparency, they demand to be included and have a voice, and they demand to be recognized. Millennials live in a world where the convergence of real life and their social media lives exist partially online in a very real way—it's not just like "oh that's online, it doesn't matter," it's real and important.
>
> They are inundated with a massive amount of content, and in order to keep up and participate must balance consumption with interacting with friends. Based on these evolving social norms, Millennials have a lot of stuff they feel they need to be doing online and may not always be interested in what you have to say, even if you spend six months researching what's relevant to them.

Schell goes on to say something that is not only true for marketing to Millennials but also could be a battle cry for social media marketing in general: "The way that smart brands can really bubble to the top is actually not broadcast out what they think is relevant and interesting, but instead participate and weave into those communities that can really push the message out and circulate it in a more natural way."

Again, not every organization or brand is able to have such a clearly defined segment. MTV's focus shows us what can be done if we take the time to immerse ourselves in our audiences. In the online space, it isn't even enough to just engage one-on-one but to do so within the social space. People within communities develop norms of behavior and dialogue; to connect effectively, you have to have an understanding of those norms. This often requires a comprehensive study of the communities in question. Scott Briggs at Alterian recently presented Alterian's process for researching within online communities using online ethnography:

► Collect social media conversations for the themes created in the research phase
► Create a conversation matrix to segment your data set by categories and themes
► Examine and quantify what is important and relevant to the target audience
► Analyze data by conversation, domain, and author within each category

Archetypal Roles in Communities
Psychologist Paul Moxnes (http://www.moxnes.com/) has suggested the roles that are played out in groups, and thus communities, fall into archetypes that he calls *deep roles* (Figure 7.1). They

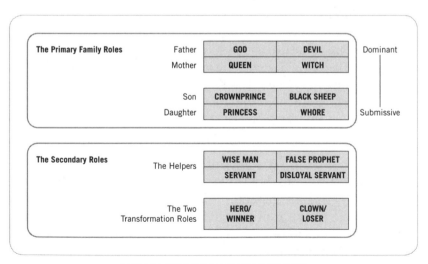

FIGURE 7.1 Paul Moxnes's role archetypes

are based on the family structure. Each of the main roles—father, mother, son, daughter, helpers—and the transformational roles have both positive and negative aspects.

You may find that the roles are not quite so black and white in particular communities, or that the roles need to be stretched. For instance, we find that a common role is that of the critic, whom we might be able to see as the false prophet. But in this case, this person is not being malevolent, instead providing value to the community by always being blatantly honest, to a fault. Still, understanding that communities are composed of people who often fill archetypal roles can help you to see community activities in terms of patterns and possibly even suggest actions for your brand to take in that community.

Ambassadors and Advocates

Within the marketing industry, people disagree about what constitutes a *brand ambassador* as opposed to a *brand advocate*. In either case, there are four main dimensions to ambassadors and advocates:

1. Recognition
2. Internal or external
3. Compensation
4. Autonomy

Of course, the term *ambassador* was originally used to designate the highest-ranking person on a diplomatic mission. Today we also have goodwill ambassadors and even cultural ambassadors. It isn't uncommon to hear statements like, "everyone in the company should be an ambassador," meaning that everyone should represent the organization in a positive light.

The fundamental differentiator between the two roles—ambassador and advocate—is that a brand ambassador is officially recognized by the brand and is given some sort of imprimatur. In the world of international diplomacy, an ambassador officially represents a country to another country. Anyone, on the other hand, can be a brand advocate. In our marketing efforts, both groups can be engaged to different ends. We can also encourage someone to be a brand advocate with monetary or other forms of compensation.

It's worth differentiating these two roles, as programs based on each can have very different outcomes and end value. If an organization is going to grant someone credentials or official recognition, a certain level of intimacy would be assumed. You'd probably want to give those individuals special access to inside information and perhaps even training. Also, it's probably not a short-term relationship.

Many companies are fortunate enough to have a cadre of individuals who are enthusiastic, perhaps even wildly enthusiastic, about their brands. Imagine harnessing the power of those individuals—perhaps providing them with special tools and information to do an even better job of spreading their enthusiasm for your brand. These people could be given special access to the CEO, or provided with tours of facilities, or provided with early glimpses of products in the works, if not actual products.

Ambassadors may also receive monetary compensation or other perks. They might be given a great deal of autonomy in what they say or write about the brand, or they might be given very definite parameters. The effectiveness of one approach over another will typically depend on your industry. For instance, some brands enjoy a high level of brand allegiance and can avoid compensating ambassadors with anything more than access to special information. A brand that doesn't inspire a high level of allegiance may need to provide monetary compensation.

Ekaterina Walter, of Intel, believes that monetary compensation creates a different type of relationship—not one that lends itself to wild enthusiasm. By giving special access to products or to an organization's leadership, she says, "it's saying, 'we respect you and we respect that relationship and we will show you behind the curtains, we will provide you access to something that not everybody else has.' It probably is some sort of payment, but you know, how you do it and the way you do it is, I think, what matters."

Mack Collier agrees. "Brand ambassadors, advocates, fans, whatever you want to call them, absolutely want to be compensated," he said. "But a lot of times, they don't want money. What they want is access to the brand. They want to be able to say that 'I'm one of 50 people in the world that saw this new product for my favorite brand before anyone else.'" Giving people special access to leadership, new products, or other perks will have a lot more impact than money. If you did pay someone $1,000, for instance, that money would soon be gone, with no guarantee of creating a lasting emotional attachment to the brand. A memory or bragging rights, however, will endure.

There are two main types of brand ambassador programs, the *internal brand ambassador program*, made up of employees and individuals within the organization, and the *customer brand ambassador program*, made up of nonemployees from outside the organization. The roles of these two types of programs can be quite different, so much so that it's often worth running both. In all cases, the people in the program should be enthusiastic and positive representatives of the brand.

Internal Brand Ambassador Program

An internal brand ambassador program can be a way of including employees throughout the organization in your social media efforts. This group of people can include your blog writers and Twitter, Facebook, LinkedIn, and other social media platform participants. Provide them with training and even a training guide covering the organization's social media policies and voice. If you're looking to integrate the whole organization into social media, start with marketing and then set up a brand ambassador (BA) program for other employees.

How a program like this gets rolled out to employees will vary by organization. Participation may be voluntary or assigned through departments. Some organizations don't allow employees to engage in social media on behalf of the organization unless they've been through training.

Consider rolling out a BA program in phases, and start small. For instance, 12 participants each blogging once a quarter would provide a new blog post weekly.

Think through the goals of the program. For example, is the goal to foster internal thought leadership, or is it to increase external interactions with customers?

Customer Brand Ambassador Program

Your approach to a customer BA program will depend on your brand and the target ambassadors. For instance, brands as beloved as Harley-Davidson and Coca-Cola generally don't have to provide monetary compensation to ambassadors (though Coca-Cola did pay students involved in its college campus program that was implemented by marketing firm Momentum Worldwide in 2008).

In Coca-Cola's Expedition 206 campaign, winners of a contest were provided travel expenses. The winning "happiness ambassadors" travelled the world talking to people about happiness and then shared their adventures using social media, photography, and video. In this campaign, Coca-Cola created an event that could be documented and shared through social media and traditional press while at the same time aligning its brand with a core passion: happiness.

There are many companies that pay brand ambassador program participants with money or merchandise in exchange for blog posts or social media posts. Other programs are simply thinly disguised commissioned sales programs.

Another approach to BA programs is to make no demands on participants whatsoever but rather to invite people into the program, give them gifts, and allow them access to leadership. This approach would be likely to create an environment where the BAs will want to speak on your behalf.

Autonomy

The amount of control that organizations are willing to cede to brand ambassadors varies widely. In the application form to become a brand ambassador for the Sears Outlet program, applicants must agree to notify the company before they post a negative blog or review, giving Sears a chance to remedy the problem. On one hand, this requirement seems pretty reasonable; on the other hand, it could be seen as indicating a lack of transparency and honesty. Participants in brand ambassador programs should be encouraged, if not required, to disclose their participation when blogging or otherwise promoting the brand.

In ceding more control to brand ambassadors, we are moving from a command-and-control mode to an enable-and-facilitate mode.

Community Managers

Generally speaking, a community manager is a person who runs the social media communications of an organization. In larger organizations, there might be a community manager for each platform. In smaller organizations, one person might be responsible for the blog, Twitter, Facebook, Quora, and other social platforms, as well as for coaching other people in the organization on the use of social media.

Community managers are responsible for encouraging communities to grow, through nurturing or, when necessary, cajoling. Even in the microcosm of a blog's comments, a good community manager will know how to draw people into the conversation like the host of a nineteenth-century literary salon.

Community managers should be good listeners who know when to step in and nudge a conversation along. They should be aware of the larger organizational social media vision and goals and engage in activities to help make them a reality. At the same time, they must advocate for the organization and the brands.

IN REAL LIFE (IRL) CONNECTIONS

When the phrase "in real life" is used in contrast to social media, there are often voices of protest, "but social media *is* real life." Perhaps the phrase should have been "in *physical* reality." Either way, there is a power in bringing connections that were hitherto nurtured in online media to a real face-to-face meeting. Having already shared ideas and knowing someone from a photograph, however small, can be an immediate ice-breaker.

Design Social Media Activities That Branch Off into IRL

In Twitter, the simple act of using a hashtag (#, or pound sign) before a word can instantly make a person part of a vibrant online community. Anyone can become a "member" simply by tweeting with the hashtag for a group, like #Latism, a group focused on Hispanic marketing, and #usguys, a 24-7 Twitter group loosely formed on Internet marketing.

In the #usguys Twitter group, members typically shout out to one another about #coffee and #wine, the weather, and other social grooming–type topics. But they also have modestly planned impromptu meetings across the world. Much like Rotarian business travelers, members let the group know when they're going on the road, and meet-ups are formed. Some of these meetings have led to job offers, freelance assignments, and perhaps even a few romances.

Take Advantage of Wispy Communities

Gary Alan Fine and Lisa-Jo van den Scott define *wispy communities* as "worlds of action that are temporary, limited in time and space, and have the potential of being displaced by other more insistent identities." While members' identification with wispy communities is less salient than with more persistent groups, strong emotional ties can form quickly.

For marketers, communities that form around brands might be wispy communities. But some wispy communities, such as Woodstock or Burning Man, produce strong emotional bonds. These bonds can allow us to create more value in our work with these communities.

For instance, too often marketers produce swag that simply advertises the brand. Considering how powerful "in real life" (IRL) events are for many participants, swag that commemorates the event is much more likely to be treasured. By combining our brands with events, giveaway mementos help create an emotional bond between our brand and our customers.

You can also design promotions around potential or planned events, such as conferences, concerts, political rallies, or parades— all great opportunities to make use of social media.

✓ CHECKLIST

- ☐ Determine if the event has a hashtag or event page.
- ☐ Find out who the players are and connect with them.
- ☐ Start talking about the event early on—connect with everyone.
- ☐ Be present in social media during and after the event.
- ☐ Incentivize people to connect with your team at the event.
- ☐ Find ways to commemorate participatory events.

CHAPTER 8

CHASING THE WHALES
GOING FOR THE INFLUENCERS

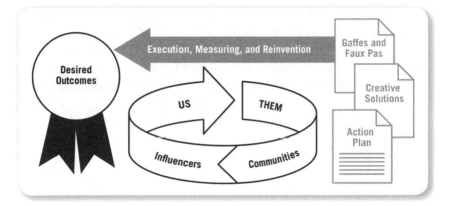

THE LINCHPIN OF MARKETING

The study of influence has always been a pillar of marketing. But before the advent of social media, we were dealing with influence in an environment in which we were truly removed from our customers. It was as though we were stuffing a message into a bottle, tossing it into the ocean, and hoping it would wash up on some distant shore, where someone, *the right someone*, would pick it up and read the message. Thanks to social media, a whole boat full of those customers has arrived, and we're all sitting down to one big beach party together. Suddenly, much of what has been learned about influence over the years has become even more relevant.

Too often it's been the dark side of humanity that has precipitated the study of influence. We struggle to understand how 22-year-old Lynndie England from Frankfort, Kentucky, a onetime member of the Future Farmers of America, could have been influenced to take part in the sexual assault on prisoners at Abu Ghraib prison in Iraq in 2004. Not too surprisingly, she said she felt that not participating would cost her the affection of a major influencer in her life, her boyfriend, one of the other guards encouraging her participation. We wonder how the 909 members of the Jonestown Massacre of 1978 could possibly have been led to take their own lives, in some cases after having killed their own children.

Influence. The word has at its root a suggestion of a flowing in. It has its origins in astrology, with the notion that a god or other unseen powers are affecting life and destiny. The fourteenth-century scholar Themon Judaeus described influence as "a certain quality or power diffused through the whole world," noting that unlike light, influence was capable of moving through metal and stone.[1] In the old movies, Bela Lugosi's Dracula could simply look into his victims' eyes and bid them to do his will. That was some serious influence. If only it were that easy. One way or another, in wielding influence, we aim to get someone to do what we want him to do.

Which is why influence is a linchpin in marketing. How is it that a person comes to buy a Honda as opposed to a Toyota, or a Pepsi instead of a Coke? Why does Mrs. Smith at 323 Elm Street vote for Senator Jones instead of Senator Miller? The answers are rarely simple. Think of a chessboard as an analogy: a board bearing a mere 64 spaces and holding just 32 pieces yields thousands of possible openings and variations. Similarly, there are endless possible ways that people bump up against information and influence.

Let's assume for a minute that you're *not* a Fuller Brush Man trying to sell hairbrushes to bald men, that, instead, as a twenty-first-century marketer, you're endeavoring to help bridge markets to your company's offerings. The need for your product exists, but the marketplace hasn't been quick to pick up on its value. In the midst of all of the noise and messages that bombard consumers daily, they're just not seeing how your offering will fulfill their needs and desires.

A big part of our job is to help the market perceive the value in our offerings. We don't want to be pushy; we just want to give a little nudge. We wish to exert *influence*. But how? Many factors impact influence. A great deal of influence research has been conducted over the years, and some major buckets of it are worth becoming familiar with if we want to be more effective in social media marketing.

WE FAVOR OUR GROUPS

Perhaps reflecting the mass bewilderment at how one very charismatic man could be the source of so much human misery, the years after World War II saw an explosion in influence studies. One of the pioneering social psychologists endeavoring to make sense of those horrible influences was Henri Tajfel, a Polish Jew who was studying in France at the outbreak of the war. After volunteering for the French army, Tajfel was captured by the Germans but survived as a prisoner of war. On returning home to Poland after the war, Tajfel found that not a single member of his family had survived the Holocaust.

Several of Tajfel's studies gave proof to the idea of *in-group bias*, or the tendency for people to give preferential treatment to others in their own group, even if that group's formation is somewhat arbitrary. In Tajfel's minimal group studies, done in the early 1970s, a group of teenage boys was divided into two subgroups based on whether they had overestimated or underestimated the number of dots projected onto a screen. After being divided into these subgroups, the boys were asked to allocate money to the other boys. By and large, there was a clear pattern of in-group favoritism. I recently saw this phenomenon in real life when I was at a conference where a task was assigned to each table. After a bit of brainstorming, a representative from each table stood and presented his or her table's ideas, whereupon the people at each table cheered. It had, in the course of an hour, become Table 6 versus Table 5!

The feeling of "my team" can arise quickly, even when the team is based on arbitrary criteria. The dark side of this phenomenon is prejudice and discrimination. In fact, the reason Tajfel called his studies *minimal group* is that they demonstrated the smallest group necessary for discrimination to occur.

Tajfel, along with his student John C. Turner, went on to develop the theory of *social identity*, which seeks to explain how individuals' sense of self is based on their notions of the groups they think they belong to. He discovered that in order to increase their own sense of self-worth, people increase the value of their groups. For instance: *my* school is the *best* school; *my* country is the *best* country. The thinking goes, "If all of these groups that I'm a part of have superlative value, it must mean *I* have significance."

PEER PRESSURE AS NORMATIVE INFLUENCE

Hans Christian Andersen's story "The Emperor's New Clothes," based on a medieval tale, was published in 1837. It would be almost another hundred years before psychologists would provide empirical support for the folk wisdom that people are strongly influenced by the opinions of those around them, even to the point of not seeing what is plainly before them or, as in the case of the emperor, seeing what is *not* there.

Like Tajfel, Solomon Asch was a Polish Jew, but fortunately he emigrated to the United States well before the ascendancy of the Nazi Party. Asch designed experiments in which subjects were told that they were taking a vision test. They were shown two cards. On the first was a vertical line, and on the second, three lines, one of which was the same length as the line on the first card.

The subjects were then asked to identify, out loud, which line on the second card matched that on the first card. The answer was fairly obvious, so much so that in a control group, only one out of 35 subjects answered incorrectly.

But when the experimenters introduced "stooges"—subjects who were actually in on the experiment, instructed to answer incorrectly—most of the subjects gave wrong answers as well, concurring with the group. Experimenting with different group sizes, Asch observed that the more people stated the wrong fact, the more a subject was apt to conform.

A study in 2005 using functional magnetic resonance imaging (fMRI) showed that when people conform to a wrong answer, there is a spike of activity in the area of the brain pertaining to spatial awareness; in other words, the subjects' perception of reality is actually affected. On the other hand, if a subject resists joining group consensus, brain activity is consistent with that of a person dealing with conflicting information and social isolation.[2]

This desire to fit in is called *normative conformity*. Another type of influence is *majority influence*, which exists where there is a need to conform to group pressure. In the classic movie *Twelve Angry Men*, Henry Fonda did *not* succumb to majority influence but instead was able to exert his own influence, which resulted in the defendant's acquittal.

There is also a strong human compulsion to be right, called *informational conformity* or *internalization*, which is a big part of why people can get so worked up in arguments. A quick way to alienate someone is to say, "You're wrong."

Herd mentality is often referred to as *social proof.* Yawning, coughing, and laughing along with the canned laughter of television sitcoms are some simple examples. As we go about our daily lives, we may find ourselves unexpectedly and unwittingly affected by the power of social proof in very mundane ways. For example, if a group of people look up at the sky, almost any bystander will have a strong urge to look up at the sky as well.

What can we do with this knowledge? There are various ways to leverage social proof in social media marketing. One popular way is to show activity. For instance, when a blog post has been commented upon many times, new visitors will be more inclined to leave comments themselves. Many blogs show how often they've been retweeted, which encourages more retweeting. On the flip side, having few responses from other people online can have a negative social proof effect.

This is why a lot of websites and social accounts enjoy a "rich get richer" effect: when there is significant social proof, it can help drive more conformity, which in turn drives even more. It has been shown that commercials actually get more callers by saying, "If operators are busy, please call again." Similarly, when we see a line around the block for that popular new nightclub, we feel we're missing out on something great, and queue up.

APPEARANCE OF AUTHORITY

One of Asch's doctoral students, Yale psychologist Stanley Milgram, actually created an experiment in which a crowd of people looked up at the sky. The study for which he is best known, though, involved test subjects who were instructed to administer increasingly strong electrical shocks to another person. While the electrical shocks turned out to be fake, the results were not: the study clearly demonstrated that the majority of people will inflict pain and suffering on another person when encouraged or told to do so by someone perceived to be in a position of authority.

A positive, nonsadistic takeaway for online marketers? Whenever feasible, you should look to demonstrate authority on your topics. That doesn't mean your team needs to dress in white lab coats for your avatar photos. Instead, look to webinars, tweetchats, and white papers to create an aura of authority. On business-to-business websites, testimonials not only help to create social proof but also establish authority, particularly when recognizable logos are involved.

Milgram is also famous for his *small world experiments* wherein participants were asked to forward a letter to an acquaintance they thought would most likely, through her contacts, help the letter reach its final recipient. In most cases within the United States, the letter made its way to the final recipient with about three connections. The study is often cited in the support of the "six degrees of separation" concept that has become popular in movies and literature.

TWO-STEP INFLUENCE AND SMALL GROUPS

While Nazi atrocities spurred much influence research, the powerful propaganda machines of both the Allies and the Axis, and the growth of big media after World War II, contributed to a strong curiosity about the role that media plays in influencing people to buy products, choose movies, and vote for politicians.

In 1945 a group of sociologists led by Paul F. Lazarsfeld descended on Decatur, Illinois, to conduct what was to become known as the *Decatur Study*. Before the sociologists departed, they interviewed more than 800 women over a period of time to determine how they were influenced in their decisions on a variety of activities, including shopping, choosing movies, and voting. The results of the study (delayed for nearly a decade due to infighting among the sociologists) were finally published in 1955 in a landmark book, *Personal Influence*. The sociologists found that the majority of people in the study were mostly influenced by their own small groups, and that those small groups were in turn influenced by opinion leaders, or certain individuals whose opinions were highly regarded. In other words, in what has been called the two-step theory, big media's messages were filtered through an influencer or two before they reached most people. But that was right before television really became ubiquitous. "Big media," at that time, was more about magazines and newspapers. Had the study been made 10 years later, the results might have been dramatically different.

By the time that study actually saw print in the mid-1950s, the average American was viewing four to five hours of television per day! By the later 1960s, children would typically turn on the television as soon as they got home from school. Families often ate their dinners while watching *I Love Lucy* or *The Ed Sullivan Show*.

In a way, we could be seeing a return to a time, like the 1940s, when people are influenced primarily by their small groups. Except this time, it's happening online. The history of media and transportation in the last 60 years tells a story of communities becoming molecularized. It has progressively become easier for people to spend a lot more time outside of their physical communities. It's possible that with social media, communities are being knit back together, but in different forms than before, and with influencers playing a major role.

Many marketers believe that in order to make an impact, they must engage a major influencer. The Decatur Study's finding— that people are by and large more influenced by the influencers within their small groups, at least on many major issues—is an important clue for marketers using social media.

THE REALLY BIG INFLUENCERS

Back when *The Oprah Winfrey Show* was on, if you were an author who wanted to sell a lot of books, you really would have liked for Oprah to stand before her audience and tell them they should buy your book. For author Uwem Akpan, a Nigerian priest and author of *Say You're One of Them*, a collection of stories set in war-torn Africa, Oprah's endorsement resulted in over 405,000 book sales, compared to 47,500 beforehand—an 853 percent increase. If you're a performer, getting the imprimatur of Simon Fuller, the creator of *American Idol*, could launch your career. As marketers, of course, we'd like for such influencers to tell the world about *our* offerings.

While a shout-out from a celebrity like Oprah Winfrey or a public figure like Barack Obama can have a large impact, sustained change requires additional exposure. After Obama gave his famous "back to school" speech, he followed up with speeches across the country, while his administration helped to craft and promote legislation to support the initiative. Oprah Winfrey suggested books and interviewed authors, and her multifaceted business empire continued to promote her choices.

While it would be a mistake to focus only on the superinfluencers, it would also be a mistake to underestimate the importance of influencers. Some social media marketers believe that this is indeed the age of real one-on-one marketing and that consumers are crying out for that level of interactivity. The reality, however, is that marketers must still leverage limited resources. And as Martin Nowak wrote in *Super Cooperators*, "The six degrees of separation idea works in such a network because in every small group of friends there are a few people who have much wider connections, either across continents or across social divisions."[3]

In sociologist Mark Granovetter's groundbreaking book *Getting a Job*, the author makes the case that under many circumstances, it's not the people closest to you who exert the most influence but people who are further away from you in your social network. Granovetter referred to the friends and family in your immediate network as *strong ties*, as opposed to *weak ties*, those people who are only loosely connected to you. Consider the music preferences of your closest friends, whose tastes you're very likely to be familiar with. Because you've already shared ideas about music within your closest circle of friends, you're more apt to learn about new and different music from people outside of that circle.

THE FLOW OF INFLUENCE

In addition to understanding why some people are more influential than others, or why some messages seem to resonate more than others, the path of how an idea arrives can be equally important. We can begin to understand influence not only as a well-delivered message but also as the spreading of thoughts within an eco-system of influence.

Horizontal Influence

Lazarsfeld was also the lead on a study in the early 1940s that focused on the 1940 presidential election. That study determined that the influence of personal contacts played a larger part in people's decision making than what they heard on the radio or read in newspapers. At the time, this was referred to as *horizontal opinion leadership*.

Horizontal influence is prevalent across the cultural spectrum. Some influence flows more easily within a single social stratum, while other influence flows readily from one class to another, even in both directions. What the affluent are naming their children is likely to establish norms for popular names among the middle class in subsequent years, while those same affluent children will be dancing at their high school proms to music that might have originated with some of the least wealthy people in society.

In the early 1960s, organizational psychologists started to examine how influence also flows across organizations from worker to worker in what they called *lateral persuasion*. Whether referred to as lateral or horizontal, influence moves in many different directions with varying degrees of impact.

The power of influence exists throughout society, both small scale—as between a couple of friends—and large scale, as when companies work to persuade consumers to purchase their products. Within a corporation, an employee might try to get a boss to do something through indirect means, being clever and even circumspect in using persuasion tactics, while a boss wanting something from a subordinate might be more direct and demanding. Both approaches yield influence.

Our challenge in online marketing is that while one-on-one influence is most efficacious, we have to achieve a scalable effect.

Direct or Roundabout Influence

The power of influence depends heavily on its source and context. For instance, you might value a teenager's music recommendations (she's tapped into the latest trends!), but, knowing her ardor for chicken nuggets, you might hesitate before taking her restaurant recommendations. A person we admire—perhaps for her success—might have a strong influence on our decision making, while we might give less weight to the opinions of the cable man who comes to fix the Internet connection.

Influence, like value, is contextual. In many early influence studies and tests, sociologists were perplexed that some variables were extremely influential under some circumstances but not in others, sometimes even decreasing influence. Sociologists subsequently developed the Elaboration Likelihood Model (ELM), which takes into consideration sources and context of influence. This model showed that an influencer may be less important than how the topic of influence, at any moment, fits into the life of the person being influenced.

When I visit my physician, she inevitably gets around to reminding me to exercise more and eat less pizza. She reasons that at my age, the body metabolizes fat differently, and that stress-induced hormonal changes are making me more Homer Simpsonesque. The way I assimilate such cogent and logical arguments is known as *central processing.*

On the other hand, if I overhear some of my female friends admiring the fit, handsome rock star who lives down the street, I might feel equally motivated—perhaps even more so—to change my dietary and exercise habits. The consideration of this kind of indirect influence is known as *peripheral processing.* Making purchasing decisions based on your having been entertained by an advertisement, or on an admiration for the passion behind a brand's messaging about sports, are other examples of peripheral processing.

Heuristics—Processing Influence

Another theory holds that in a world where we are taking in so many influence signals, we develop internal rules, or *heuristics,* for processing those influences. One factor is how much a particular issue means to a person at any given moment. *I can't possibly analyze all the data available to me, so since I have not had any bad experiences with Brand X, and absent any other influential information, I'll just choose that over its competitors.*

Peripheral or heuristic processing is a key impact point in social media; more direct attempts to exert influence can actually backfire.

It's rare that we can clearly identify one mode of influence as being the main driver. Usually, several influencers are at work. By thinking through the various elements of influence, you might recognize opportunities that are being missed in your social campaigns, or even just consider them as a brainstorming component in improving your marketing efforts.

BEING INFLUENTIAL

As marketers, we can approach the world of influence from different angles. First, we can search out and work with influencers.

Second, we can seek to be influential. These are by no means mutually exclusive approaches. The following sections are intended as a rough guide to help you think about how you're using influence in your projects. Also, as you study the influencers in your industry, you can seek out the main drivers that help to make those individuals sources of influence. But bear in mind, there is no one-size-fits-all solution. These guidelines are meant to be more of a source of inspiration and ideas than a formula for success.

Are You Gifting?

In the earliest days of the Internet, there was a wonderful air of generosity. If a woman in Des Moines had a problem with her computer, a stranger in New Jersey would be willing to take the time to explain the solution. Spam and commercialism did their share to diminish this spirit of giving, but it didn't go away altogether—it's alive and well in social media. And it is one of the most powerful forces in influence.

Marcel Mauss was a sociologist whose 1923 book *The Gift* presented a wide range of thoughts about gifting and reciprocity. In the context of the primitive cultures Mauss observed, reciprocal gifting is a driving force in how people build relationships with one another. There is a power in the giving of gifts, and, as Mauss wrote, "The unreciprocated gift still makes the person who has accepted it inferior, particularly when it has been accepted with no thought of returning it."[4]

The world of nonprofit fund-raising has been leveraging reciprocity for some time. Whether it's a Unificationist pressing a flower into your hands at the airport, or Easter Seals sending you a solicitation accompanied by a sheet of gummed address labels, the gift significantly increases the chance that you will make a donation. The immense power of the impulse to reciprocate was the subject of a 1971 study by Dennis T. Regan.

In the experiment, subjects were ostensibly asked to participate in a study on aesthetics. There were two main test conditions. In the first, a confederate of the experimenter joined the subject in the lab as they waited for the study to begin. The confederate then left the room and returned with two bottles of soda, giving one to the test participant, unsolicited. In the second test condition, no gift was given. In both conditions, the confederate slipped a note to the subject, asking him to buy some raffle tickets. In cases where a soda was offered, the chance of a subject buying more than a single raffle ticket more than doubled.

We live in a world of reciprocity. As Robert Putnam says in *Bowling Alone*, this reciprocity is the touchstone of social capital. The notion of social capital is that there is value in social connections and the giving that occurs in those networks. This value permeates the fabric of society all around us.

As marketers, we can practice generosity within the communities we hope to influence. We shouldn't act generous, though, with the goal of direct reciprocity, but rather to help create an environment of giving. If people get the feeling that your generosity is tied directly to your need for marketing return, it will backfire. Instead, your generosity must be tied to your underlying principals.

People are constantly giving little gifts to one another. When someone clicks the "like" button or the "+1" Google Plus button, or retweets someone's tweet, he's giving a very small gift, as all those little gestures help to show social proof and have potential additive benefit for search engine optimization. Such gift giving isn't necessarily completely altruistic—there might be a sense of, "Hey, I'm liking what you just said, so *notice* me back, OK?"— but for many people, this exchange is simply made with a sense of community and sharing.

But the truth is, when someone comments on my company's blog or shares something we've posted with her friends, she *is* giving us a gift. The content building up on our pages increases our digital footprint with the search engines and, hopefully, helps to create a community in which others will want to participate. That is our gift to the community. And when a gift has been given, there is a strong compulsion to reciprocate—in our community's case, in the form of comments and sharing.

As a marketer, you might consider starting a random gift program—pulling up lists of the people who are interacting with your brand, selecting a few, and sending them each a gift. Don't ask them to tweet about it or share with their friends—you don't want the random gift to engender any sense of obligation. Send along a nice handwritten (and friendly!) note. Just imagine having been the person who received a small crystal ornament from Steuben accompanied by a handwritten note from the head of marketing simply saying, "Thank you for your joining us in our online community—just wanted you to know how much it means to us."

Are You Creating Groups?

As shown in Tajfel's experiments, when people associate themselves with a group, they are more inclined to favor other members of that group. Think through all of the touchpoints you have with your customers, and see if there are ways to draw them into a group that includes you.

On Empire Avenue, a stock market simulation social network game, participants are able to opt in to several groups based on both interests and geographical region. These groups encourage subgroup formation, which could have a strong influence over whether a person continues to play on Empire Avenue, simply because he's able to find people of similar interests. If you're a guitarist, you can find other guitarists. And if jazz is your thing, you can find jazz guitarists. The designers of Empire Avenue were capitalizing on our tendency to associate with people of like beliefs and interests.

For marketers, we should look for ways to define groups in such a way that they include both ourselves and our customers. Asking customers to join a group, club, or community presents a completely different mindset than asking them to join a mailing list. It isn't enough to simply rename your list as a group, but you must find ways to help it really function as a group or a community. Brand ambassador programs, which I discussed at greater length in Chapter 7, are another powerful way of doing this.

In approaching customers this way, it is important to avoid communicating anything other than that we belong to the same group as our customers, avoiding an us-and-them mentality. This approach is rooted in being customer-centric from the beginning, seeing the world through customers' eyes and acting from that vantage point.

Instead of using social media to get your message out to a prospective customer, think of a day in the life of that customer, and then imagine what value you can add to that day.

Are You Friendly and Likable?

Perhaps it isn't in your brand to be friendly—there are brands that celebrate aloofness and hauteur. In such a case, the friendliness factor is one element of influence that might not be available to you, although you may be able to imagine an aloofness and hauteur that might be practiced by a kindly elder aunt.

If you're not one of those too-cool-for-school brands, you need to bring as much friendliness as possible into your social media. Find people who can communicate with friendliness. If people are sour and negative, they probably aren't good candidates for social media.

See the difference between this post from the Facebook page of MINI (as in the Mini Cooper car):

> Tread lightly: though the latest adventure story on MINI Space didn't involve a flying, fire-breathing beast, it did involve an 11-mile stretch of U.S. highway with 318 steep curves—The Tail of the Dragon. Learn what takes place as MINI fans meet in Great Smoky Mountain National Park to show this legendary road which car is boss.

Compared to this post from Ford Fiesta's page:

> Stay tuned for more updates from "The FIESTA Experience" through the week. Follow our participants as they chronicle the journey of 1300 kms from Delhi-Diu in the All-New Fiesta. To book your own Test Drive of the All-New Fiesta in India . . .

There's nothing explicitly wrong with Ford's post—it's just that Mini's is just a little bit friendlier.

Are You Showing Credibility?

When I pay you with my *credit* card, you believe that you're going to get your money. If I have a *credo*, I have a certain belief that I uphold. If I have credibility, you trust and believe in me.

According to Robert Gass and John Seiter,[5] there are three primary dimensions to credibility:

- ▶ Expertise
- ▶ Trustworthiness
- ▶ Goodwill

Showing that your brand and the people associated with your brand have expertise requires a delicate touch—it can be overdone. But wherever you can share your expertise and that of your organization and the people in it, the better. Sharing advice on social media sites like Facebook and Quora that have question and answer sections presents a great opportunity.

Consider creating a thought leadership program. Using your blog as a linchpin, you can call on different people in the organization to author pieces that demonstrate authority and expertise on subjects that are relevant to your world. Those same individuals can also become guest bloggers on outside blogs, which not only helps to drive new traffic to the main blog but can also help build a web of connections between your organization and other relevant individuals.

Trustworthiness should be simple, although in some industries it can be challenging, not because the people in those industries are less trustworthy, but because they have to be more careful about how they say things. Pharma and investment banking are two good examples.

Consider this statement by Tony Hayward of BP shortly after the beginning of the Gulf oil spill in 2010: "The company will pay for any 'legitimate and objectively verifiable' claims for property damage, personal injury and commercial losses."[6]

These are obviously words provided by an attorney and aren't framed to maximize both the message and trustworthiness. Your attorneys work for you (or your company)—and if they don't give you language that is maximized for trustworthiness and friendliness, they need to go back to the drawing board. The type of legalese seen in Hayward's statement is destructive to brand equity. The use of the words "legitimate and objectively verifiable claims" demonstrates a greater concern for protecting the company than for taking responsibility for a humanitarian disaster.

During the time of the Gulf oil spill, BP shared photographs of its main command center showing banks of active video monitors. The only problem was, as someone noticed, the photographs had been digitally manipulated to show more activity on the screens than was actually taking place. It was a simple deception, but given the circumstances, deception of any sort should have been avoided at all costs. Since the explosion of social media and the kind of citizen journalism that can often reveal cover-ups, there has been a strong rallying cry for transparency from organizations. While it may not be appropriate to share all information, there is a compelling business case for practicing transparency to your organization's maximum allowable threshold: it creates a sense of trustworthiness. And in achieving that, you add another element to your influence portfolio.

——— SOCIAL MEDIA INFLUENCE TOOLS ———

After a comprehensive study of audience subsegments and their communities, I push the keys on my computer keyboard and a complete report materializes on the screen in front of me. The report shows all of the various individuals who are influential around all of the various topics that my company's work touches upon. It also shows, within those topics, where they exert that influence, the breadth of their influence, and even who influences *them*.

The program then allows me to track all of my interactions with those influencers, helping me to increase and improve my engagement with them. And finally, the program provides me with metrics on how our engagement is improving over time.

Sounds great, right? Unfortunately, this program doesn't exist. Some of the enterprise tools in existence are showing promise, but they're unable to account for degree of influence. For instance, there might be a person with 100 followers, and another with 100,000 followers. The person with fewer followers could conceivably be more influential in, say, the prom dress industry, especially if 90 of those 100 followers are prom dress designers, but the software isn't going to see this.

Then there is the issue of *type* of influence. Malcolm Gladwell, in his popular book *The Tipping Point*, suggested that in order to make something viral, at least three different types of influencers are involved: the maven (the person who really understands the subject), the connector (that person who introduces people to one another or to ideas), and the salesman (the enthusiast or cheerleader). In contrast, Klout, the rising star of popular social media influence tools, describes influencers in these dynamics:

1. Sharing versus creating.
2. Listening versus participating—this is shorthand for whether a person is active in social media or not.
3. Broad versus focused—are there many themes showing up in the person's (or organization's) social communications, or do they tend to be more focused on a few concepts?
4. Casual versus consistent.

Let's imagine a couple of scenarios in which different types of influencers come into play: I'm the CMO for Acme Prom Dresses.

We design and manufacture prom dresses that are sold in small shops across the country. These retailers purchase their dresses from a handful of companies. They go to the fashion shows or look at the catalogues, but they also make decisions based on a feeling for the trends.

Scenario 1. Acme Prom Dresses has a strong presence in social media, and we've been able to connect with at least half of our direct buyers on social media. We're involved in a weekly chat on Twitter and frequently have back-and-forth with individuals in the buyers' community. In this scenario, *we* are an influencer. A couple of weeks back, we were talking about the new trend for big colored sashes and the resurgence of the Marilyn Monroe look. Buyers say they like us, and sales reflect that.

Scenario 2. Another group of people we watch are the journalists and bloggers who cover teen fashion trends. We follow those individuals wherever they might be online, retweeting their tweets, commenting on their blogs, and engaging with them whenever possible. One of the journalists really liked a series on our blog about some trends and ended up mentioning the blog in an article in *Teen Vogue*. Many of the buyers saw that article, and, sure enough, we saw a great spike in sales.

Scenario 3. Carrie, one of our social media community managers, suggested that we add tags to all of our dresses, encouraging buyers to register their dresses on our Facebook fan page and to share their prom photos. We also featured a contest for the best prom photo, and a game wherein our Facebook fans could share those photos with their friends. Images of our dresses spread like wildfire, and because of tracking codes we included in our Facebook work, we were able to see a 17 percent increase in sales in the following season related to that effort.

These three scenarios involve different types of influencers. In order to find these individuals and make the connections we made, we had to rely on a combination of influence tools and good old-fashioned search engine research. One of the big problems there, though, is that some social platforms are closed to the search engines, resulting in a lot of manual work in spreadsheets. Social media is still a relative newcomer in the world of media, and doubtless, the necessary marketing tools will be developed. The most important concern in developing those tools is designing them in such a way that they answer the right questions—as opposed to having to develop questions to fit the tools.

It's true that social media provides marketers with the ability to see and study influence as never before. A simple message can be tracked as it is initiated, fans out across a network, then finally fizzles out or is reborn through other social networks.

——— INFLUENCER OUTREACH PROJECTS ———

In an influencer outreach project, the objective generally is to connect with influencers in the hope that they ultimately write about your brand. For instance, for one client, our objective was to build up the blog to a point where at least five of the major influencers in the industry were sharing its content with their communities. This meant that the blog content needed to be dramatically improved, and also that those influencers had to be engaged across the social media spectrum. We commenced with a renewed content strategy for the blog, writing one new significant piece every three days. At the same time, we joined a tweetchat and connected with all five influencers on Twitter. Occasionally, we would mention one of the influencers in the blog itself and bring it to the influencer's attention via Twitter. After four months, each of the five influencers was mentioning our client's brand at least once a month.

Or let's say we're working with a company that manufactures technology components for data centers. We've identified several subsegments that we'd like to work within—primarily people who manage data centers in government. In those subsegments, there are medium to key influencers that we would like to develop a relationship with, sharing information both ways, with the hope that they learn about our brand and talk about us within their networks.

By the end of the six-month period, we would like

- ▶ Four high influencers to have blogged about our latest product
- ▶ Ten medium to high influencers to comment on our blog posts at least once a week

▶ Our "share of voice" on our main topics to increase by 10 percent

For the sake of this project, high influencers are people who have at least 10,000 followers on Twitter, or bloggers of a major industry blog. Medium influencers have at least 5,000 followers on Twitter or have otherwise been identified in our influencer documentation. (How influencers are identified for the sake of any given project should be determined in the context of the organization, the competition, and the market—and is the next step).

Identifying Influencers

Identifying the subsegments was discussed in the previous chapter. With each subsegment, you can use conventional web research to discover the influencers for any particular segment. Depending on the subject, other search engines like Technorati might be helpful as well.

We begin by creating a Google search based on "'data center' + government." We'll also search "'data center' + government + blog," which might help us find blogs. On the blogs themselves, several include blog rolls, or lists of other blogs that the authors think are important. All of the results will be entered into a spreadsheet that includes a field for notes. As we go through the various sites, we'll make any notes that might help us later on. For instance, is this a single author or multiauthor blog?

If those authors also have social media profiles, we'll make note of those as well.

Adopt-an-Influencer

Once the influencers have been identified, the team will begin a systematic following of each, being sure to read their blogs, tweets, and other social media postings each day. When appropriate, the team member might comment, retweet, or even just "like" or "+1." Following influencers requires finesse; otherwise it might appear that you're just being a cyber suck-up.

Goals may vary: you might be looking for those influencers to ultimately become aware of your brand and to write about you on their own blog, or you might want them to become active participants on your site.

✓ **CHECKLIST**

Influencing, working with influencers, and understanding the elements of influence will have a central role in all of your marketing efforts. This process can act as a "taking of the pulse" for your organization's efforts with influence.

- ☐ Audit
- ☐ Create influencer dossiers
- ☐ Monitor
- ☐ Interact

Audit

The audit is an opportunity for you to review the influencers in your domain and your position in your domain as an influencer:

- ☐ Who are the influencers in your domain(s)?

Your brand and brand employees as influencers:

- ☐ How is your brand using influence?
- ☐ Are you being an authority?
- ☐ Are you gifting?
- ☐ Are you being likable?
- ☐ Are you allowing people to be part of an in-group?

Create Influencer Dossiers

- ☐ If you're using a CRM system, could you maintain a dossier on each influencer?
- ☐ Include contact points.
- ☐ Which social media platforms are they using?
- ☐ Are they blogging?
- ☐ Who is commenting on their blogs?
- ☐ Where are the influencers themselves commenting?

Monitor

- ☐ Calendarize reviewing the influencer's blog and other social media

Engage

- ☐ Carefully join the conversation when you have something meaningful to contribute.

CHAPTER 9

THE BALL IN MOTION
CREATING AN ACTION PLAN

——— THE BIGGER VISION ———

You've identified your microaudiences, researched and discovered the communities where they live, and identified the influencers in those communities. There should be several documents that resulted from those efforts:

- ▶ Goals document
- ▶ Microaudience segmentation document
- ▶ Communities document
- ▶ Influencers document

Your next step is to create an action plan for your ongoing activities and special projects. I'm often asked, "How, given the vastness and complexity of social media, can we get it all accomplished?" No matter how large your social media marketing team, your resources are still finite, and you'll need to figure out where are the best chances to make the most impact.

As author Chet Richards wrote, "A plan is an intention about how to get from where we are now to where we want to be in the future. It is an intention because although we may plan to accomplish certain things, whether we actually do, and whether they have the effects we want, depends on factors beyond our control: customers, competitors, governments, and acts of God, to name a few. The term *strategy* will be used for higher-order devices for creating and managing plans." Richards was an acolyte of the military strategist John Boyd, whom I introduced in Chapter 4. Planning and strategy map to different levels of desirable outcomes. Strategy is about a bigger vision, supported by culture and values, whereas planning maps well to objectives and metrics. According to Boyd, having a well-established strategy enables people at the implementation point to be more agile in their activities.

BRAND MAINTENANCE

A great deal of social media activities will fall into the bucket of ongoing maintenance. If you find that this is the case for your project, you can create a separate social media maintenance plan that will work alongside the action plan for special projects. For instance, ongoing maintenance items might include replying to customers on your Facebook wall or following people back on Twitter. Over time, what falls into the maintenance category will change, and various small tasks within the different channels will get added. It really depends, as so much does in social media, on your organization.

In the brand maintenance project, the focus is on creating and maintaining a general social presence. If someone looks for you in the social sphere, are you there? And if a customer should shout out your name, offering up a tidbit of criticism or praise, are you listening? It may be necessary to build up the initial social presence and connections. While many social media pundits say the quantity of social connections doesn't matter as much as the quality, a credible quantity of connections is important, if for no other reason than *social proof.* Also, social proof is relative. If a brand like

Coca-Cola had only 100,000 fans on Facebook, the brand would lack credibility on that platform. For a smaller brand, that many fans would represent a roiling success.

The following plans are essential to a maintenance project and may be relevant to your special projects as well. In project management, the documents that are expected from project tasks are referred to as outputs or artifacts. Common outputs from the maintenance project include

- Listening plan document
- Channel plan document
- Stories or case studies
- Resource pool document
- SEO research
- Blog content plan document
- Channel activities document

Listening Plan

Create a listening plan to ensure that you cover what communications you're monitoring and how you're going to filter that information to extract meaningful intelligence. If you have not chosen a listening platform or are upgrading that platform, these elements can also be used to that end as well.

- What are you listening to? Are you just monitoring for particular data, or are you also including an element of analysis, such as conversation analysis?
- Are there particular individuals or organizations that you are listening to (influencer monitoring)?
- Create a list of the brand names, competitors, and key phrases you need to be monitoring.
- Identify the channels in which you need to be listening. Will your tools be usable in new channels as they are developed?
- Identify the tools or platform that will be used for listening. If these tools have any known limitations, include them in this plan.

As you think through your vision, goals, and objectives, consider how your listening plan will support your larger strategy.

Resource Pool

Whether your social media team comprises one individual, 10 people in separate locations, or everyone in the company, create a spreadsheet showing how much time you can expect from each individual. Be sure to consider downtime, training time, and any other demands on any given individual's time. Your resources determine your velocity: without sufficient resources, you may need to extend a project over a longer period of time.

The resource pool document (Table 9.1) can include a breakdown of each individual's capabilities and strengths. If you are also using an outsourced team, work with team members to identify how much actual time your budget translates to. You should also include any people outside the marketing team who can commit to any particular piece of work.

TABLE 9.1 Resource Pool Document

October 2012				
NAME	WEEKLY MAINTENANCE TIME	WEEKLY SPECIAL PROJECT AVAILABILITY	TOTAL HOURS AVAILABLE	SPECIAL SKILLS
Joseph	10	20	30	Video
Mary	10	20	30	Sound editing
Frank	10	20	30	Incredible on Twitter
Outsourced Team	0	70	70	Focusing on influencer outreach project
Sales Department	8	0	8	Blogging

Consider that people are not typically 100 percent productive. Time spent on breaks, training, non-task-specific meetings, and other such time is nonproductive inasmuch that it does not directly further project tasks. Different roles will have different percentages of productivity. In our own shop, we anticipate about 60 to 75 percent productivity in a 40-hour week. Thus, each resource can contribute about 24 to 30 hours of productivity per week to projects.

This resource pool document will be your guide in creating a proposed activity map for the organization. It doesn't mean that you can't be agile and respond to new opportunities—just that your overall work is structured.

CHANNEL MAPPING

There are many reasons you might to choose to focus your efforts on one or more particular social media platforms. Obvious reasons include the size and activeness of any given community or the presence of a certain market segment. When doing an influencer project, your choice might be based on where those influencers are most active. If you have developed a credible number of connections on Facebook, for instance, it might be more advantageous to redirect efforts on *Huffington Post*, where there might be more potential for one-on-one conversations.

Your choice of channels and the effort you devote to each should align with what you're trying to accomplish. Usually, if the organization has not already established a robust social media presence, the initial phase will be focused on creating profiles on all relevant platforms. At the very least, doing so will prevent you from losing the ability to use your brand name on any platform. Table 9.2 shows how a company might allocate efforts to the various social channels over a time period. If you're using the Scrum method of managing your social media project, these choices are made in the Sprint planning meeting.

TABLE 9.2 Allocation of Efforts to Social Media Channels

CHANNEL NAME	PERCENTAGE OF OVERALL EFFORT	HOURS	MAIN OBJECTIVES FOR THIS TIME PERIOD	TOTAL HOURS AVAILABLE: 500
Blog	14%			
Facebook	60%	120		
Twitter	10%			
YouTube	10%			
Quora	1%			
Flikr	1%			
LinkedIn	1%			
Empire Ave	1%			
Foursquare	2%			
	=100.00%			

While we're developing our engagement with any particular platform, we go through four phases: identity work, making connections, creating content, and engagement (Figure 9.1).

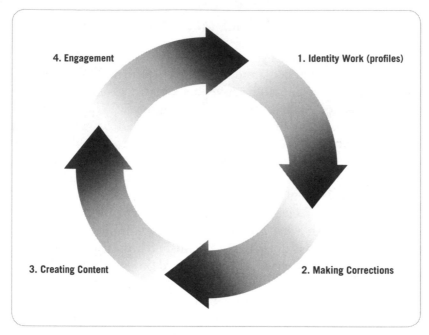

FIGURE 9.1 Four Phases of Developing Engagement

1. **Identity work.** Ensure that your profiles accurately reflect your brand, brand personality, and brand voice. In your monthly maintenance plan, include a review of all profiles; place a reminder on the calendar to return to profiles periodically to make any relevant updates.
2. **Making connections.** How connections are made differs from channel to channel. In Twitter, making connections involves following people of interest, influencers, or following back individuals who have followed your profile. You can use your website or even paid advertising to create connections or to help build up connections. Often the publishing of content helps to attract relevant people. In the case of your blog, you're likely to be using other social media and search engine optimization (SEO) to help bring those people in as connections. While you should strive to interact with all sorts of individuals, at some point, one-on-one contact isn't feasible; you have to create an environment in which others are communicating on your behalf.
3. **Creating content.** You don't want to be a "fire hose," or someone who publishes too much content. Some marketers

maintain that publishing once a day to Facebook, for instance, is adequate, while others might do so several times a day. Publishing on a microblog format like Twitter might permit a couple of dozen posts on any particular day, and if you're involved with Twitter chats, even more. It is certainly permissible to post even more when you're communicating one-on-one, nonpublicly, which is more about *engagement*.

4. **Engagement.** In one-on-one engagement with members of a community, you're not as restricted as in general content publishing. You can't make too many one-on-one engagements. Marketer and author Scott Stratten presented a chart that shows that in more than 80,000 tweets, over 78 percent went directly to other users and were not broadcast to the world. If the person doing the engagements logs them into a spreadsheet (unless you have a program to manage your social media work), you will start to connect with a community of people who begin to communicate back.

If yours is a community in the hundreds of thousands or even the millions, responding and engaging with your social media audience is going to require a lot of maintenance. Alternatively, as with organizations with smaller communities, you can loop through your microaudience segments, periodically experimenting with different segments. In the process, you'll be doing the homework for other marketing endeavors, finding where you might have unexpected success with any particular microgroup. After a profile is created, cycle through the other three phases in a loop.

MAP ACTIVITIES TO SOCIAL PYRAMID

That pyramid used in Chapter 2 to describe the patterns of various social media platforms (see Figure 2.1) can be put to use again in mapping activities to those platforms.

Groups

If the channel allows for group interactions, you can become an active participant, with the objective of making your voice ubiquitous within those groups. When you belong to and participate in a group, you develop relationships with people who are relevant to your brand. Instead of finding and interacting with people one at a time, you're dealing with a larger pool; thus people who are more inclined to be interested in you will emerge. In business-to-business marketing, this might even be a leading tactic. But know your place in the group—you don't want to overwhelm the group and alienate people.

You can identify and join groups that are in themselves aligned with your passion points. For example, if my product addressed sustainability and we had decided to lead with that passion point, we could join groups that discuss sustainability. As search engine optimization becomes more and more based on relevant links from sites with content that correlates to yours, you gain extra value when those community members link to your content.

Gaming

There are two main ways that we can participate in gamification elements: one, we can create gamified content, or two, we can join existing game environments. You can even bring a sense of games to nongame environments. I could, for example, announce an impromptu contest on YouTube: whoever uploads the best video response will be featured on our blog. It's usually a good idea to check with your legal team to ensure that you are compliant with any laws in your industry that might address contests. It isn't uncommon to use a third-party service to administer contests, as they often have compliance issues covered.

Curation

Curation can be a whole tactical endeavor in and of itself that spans channels or is channel specific. By searching out and sharing content that is relevant to your communities, your brand can come to be seen as a trusted and reliable source of information around your chosen passion points. Conduct a separate curation brainstorming sessions where you consider your audiences and ask, "What type of content would enhance our standing in this community?" Curating content can be a particularly valuable tactic when a marketing team doesn't have adequate resources to create a significant amount of original content.

Gifting

Gifting is innate to social media, although much of the time, at a hardly noticeable scale. Retweeting, "liking," or G+'ing are all examples of a small gift. Community managers should actively work to build gifting into their daily activities. We've also designed activities around actual gifts that we've given to targeted influencers or simply to individuals who have engaged with us a lot on social platforms. These small gifts are unexpected and often prompt a lot of social noise from recipients.

Relationships

In Facebook, it's making friends. In Twitter, it's being followed. In Google Plus, it's being put into circles. On your blog, it's having people signed up to receive e-mail notice of blog updates. In countless other social media platforms, it's simply being on the same platform. Whatever form it takes, connection making is that virtual handshake wherein a social tie is formalized.

At the beginning of a social media marketing program or following the establishment of new account profiles, making connections might be your sole focus; as a marketing program matures, making connections remains an ongoing activity.

Make the first move. Connect with people who are interesting to the brand. There are differences in how you connect with people on the different platforms.

Some brands on Twitter have large followings, and they follow people back. Ford Motor Company (@Ford) has over 79,000 followers and is following over 33,000. Coca-Cola has over 360,000 followers and follows over 66,000 back. Since there is no realistic way to actually read the Twitter stream of so many people, the follow-back is a symbolic gesture. On Twitter, you don't need to follow people back to engage with them, and if you start following some back, are you at risk by not following others back? Can following someone be seen as a tacit approval? Could following someone, then unfollowing them later, actually cause ill will?

Some brands avoid these questions by not following anyone. Levi's is followed by over 50,000 people (@levis) but only follows a handful of individuals, all within the Levi's organization.

Companies that don't follow back might be missing an opportunity. The follow-back is a microgift. Of course, the brand can still mention someone in a tweet. Is it a scalability issue? As Adam Evers of Famous Dave's of America said, "We haven't seen really any increase in engagement. Mostly just a nice gesture." Scott Monty of Ford said that at one time, they followed everyone back who followed Ford, but they relied on a third-party service that was not always reliable. "Now we simply follow people back who we find interesting, or when we need someone to direct message us some information. Otherwise, we use Twitter by searching for mentions of our company, our products, and other key terms that would make sense for engagement."

The entire issue is moot on Facebook, because when a person "likes" a page, there is no expectation of reciprocity.

Whatever the platform, by building in some rules for the social media team, questions about connection etiquette can be managed more easily. For instance, you could decide to follow back or reciprocate a connection based on preset criteria. Evers of Famous Dave's says that the company decides whether to follow someone based on a combination of Klout score, follower count, and relevance in real life. Other brands have chosen even less strict criteria, such as whether the person actually communicates one-on-one with others, isn't a spammer, and uses a photo on his or her profile.

Make sure to ask people to connect with the business at the point of contact. Social media often seems at its richest when connections and conversation go from online into real life and then back again. Getting our customers from our live interactions into our online communities is incredibly valuable and possibly one of the easiest opportunities that is constantly being missed by businesses. It isn't enough, though, to simply put up a sign that says, "Follow Us on Facebook." Hand out cards. Ask to connect with people. Don't just ask them to care about you, but take an active enough role in caring about your customers that you want to follow, friend, and encircle them. Provide them with an incentive—a reason to care—to join you in the social space. Again, it's going to be easier if you're operating from a passion point as opposed to a promotional stance: "What social media are you using? We'd love to connect with you so that we can send you some special offers and show that we love you."

Conversations

You have to decide where and how you want to become involved in conversations because as an activity, it isn't scalable. It's often best to engage in conversations within the structure of an influencer-based campaign. You can also think in terms of being a great party host: how do you help others make conversation on your behalf? One way is to not jump in and hit the reply button (unless it's a customer care issue that needs to be addressed immediately), but, if possible, to let your community create the conversation. You enter at important moments to keep the flow going.

Presence

Some social platforms indicate to other users when a particular user is online. Brands can take advantage of this feature by having team members constantly logged in and listening, thus highlighting the fact that you are present.

Reputation

On social platforms that allow users to develop reputations for their participation in the community, marketers have the opportunity to contribute often and to become more visible. A profile can gain points or other tokens of status for participation. For instance, on SEOmoz, users receive points when they like or share items.

BLOG MANAGEMENT

A blog can be considered the center of the social universe. A social media program could be executed without a blog, but to do so would be like entering a boxing ring with an arm tied behind your back. A topnotch corporate blog can be as challenging as publishing a print magazine; in addition to issues such as editing and content management, there's the added layer of community management.

The content of your blog should be dictated by your overall vision and goals. If you wish to attain and hold a position of thought leadership in extruded widgets, then it's natural to have a blog about extruded widgets. Furthermore, your blog should be focused not on extruded widgets themselves but on your passion points.

As with all your social media activities, your plans are going to be shaped by the resources available to you, whether that's employee time or outside resources. In many organizations, it's possible to tap blogging resources outside of the marketing team, while in others, blog authorship must come from within those ranks. If your team is limited in resources, capitalize on expertise from other places in the company.

Audio or video-based interviews can add another level of value, as they can be transcribed and used as the basis for textual blog posts (which also helps SEO); they can also be published to social media sites.

There is no one-size-fits-all setup for managing your blog. Managing the multiauthor blog is somewhat akin to publishing a magazine, except instead of creating discrete issues with a particular deadline, the blog rolls out continuously. The overall category structure of your blog should provide you with the basis for a content plan. It's possible that some of your categories are more important than others, in which case you don't want an evenly balanced blog.

By doing keyword research early on, you can identify main topics around your passion points. You can then build out a robust set of categories. Veteran blogger Liz Strauss suggests considering your categories as your table of contents and your tags as your index.

By creating a blog content plan, you can ensure that keyword research has been done in advance of the writing assignment and that blog authors are able to plan their work. It will also help to ensure that your blog categories are as balanced as needed.

TABLE 9.3 Blog Content Plan

CATEGORY	PROPOSED BLOG TOPIC	AUTHOR	PROJECTED PUBLISH DATE	KEY PHRASES
Tropical Experience	Tropical mixed drinks	D'Arcy	2/12/2012	Banana and strawberry daiquiri, tropical drinks
Caribbean Vacations	How to pack for a cruise	Ivkovic	2/19/2012	Packing for a cruise
European Vacations	Vegetarians on vacation in Spain	Legnini	2/23/2012	Vegetarians, vegans, Spain, vacation

A blog content plan also allows people working in particular channels to research and discover conversations taking place around the upcoming topics. For the example in Table 9.3, our social media worker might join Twitter chats or Facebook chats relating to eating vegetarian. He could even tip his hand and let people know he's about to write such a blog and ask if anyone has any ideas. Should anyone contribute ideas, the blogger can then mention her in the blog and have cause to give the contributor a shout-out.

If you're involved with an influencer program, you can even craft blog topics that might specifically appeal to certain influencers and their audiences. Interviews are a great opportunity to involve an influencer and create fresh content. It's not a bad idea to send a gift, or at least a handwritten thank-you note, to someone you've interviewed.

RULES OF ENGAGEMENT

Whether your social media marketing team is part of an agency or within corporate walls, creating case studies offers many benefits. Unfortunately, people tend to view case studies as something you do when you're trying to sell yourself. However, they also can serve as a repository for useful bits of knowledge. By initiating a case study at the beginning of any project, the task becomes much easier, if not effortless. Start by documenting the following:

- ► Problem or challenge
- ► Proposed solution or tactic

Then it's simply a matter of putting a review date on the calendar to document the results. If the results aren't what you were aiming for, it's still incredibly valuable to have documentation to help you identify why a project didn't work as planned.

This is the tactical plan:

- ► Identify social platforms
- ► Determine resources
- ► Create a content plan
- ► Allocate effort

Syndicating Content to Multiple Social Platforms

Many tools allow marketers to post content across multiple platforms with a certain degree of automation. The syndication of content to multiple social platforms needs to be approached with caution. There might be instances where it makes sense—particularly where time and resources are limited and there are important messages to get out. Otherwise, syndicating content will not endear you to your social community; in fact, it can alienate people.

In many instances, your organization may be connecting with people on more than one social media platform. If you're focusing on key influencer work, it can be enriching to connect with those influencers across platforms. Posting the same content on each of those platforms offers little value.

Social Media Automation

Much of the time, though, the risks of automated posts may have more to do with setting expectations. When the Seattle Police Department experimented with tweeting emergency calls, many followers were delighted. Others, however, felt it was a violation of the social media relationship. Blogger Linda Thomas wrote, "The Seattle social media community is a family. Today, the SPD was a noisy uncle at the dinner table who was only talking about himself—in incoherent sentences at that—and refusing to acknowledge that there are others in the room."[1]

Brands often try to overcome the scalability issues in social media by using tools that allow for posting the same item to the same platform throughout the day, in the likelihood of being able to catch different groups of people at different times. If you're not constantly monitoring responses, you might not be there if someone responds to the post, and then that person will understand that you've used a tool to time a post. In some communities, this practice is frowned upon. Again, really know your community. Perhaps even ask the community members how they feel about your auto posting at different times or across different platforms.

Maintain Your Engagement

The *propinquity effect* is the tendency for people to bond with others that they frequently encounter. In marketing, there is a foggy area between awareness and top-of-mind awareness. One of the great advantages of social media is that it puts us in close proximity with our customers. If you stay away from any particular community for too long, you're not going to get that effect! You'll need to experiment with each community in which you participate. In some communities, if you're absent for two weeks, there will be people asking, "Who's the new guy?" In other communities, an absence of a few weeks might be perfectly fine.

✔ CHECKLIST

Possible Plans

☐ Listening plan document

☐ Channel plan document

☐ Resource pool document

☐ Blog content plan document

☐ Channel activities document

CHAPTER 10

ARE WE THERE YET?
MEASURING YOUR PROGRESS

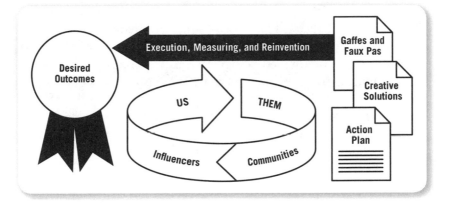

IDENTIFYING METRICS

In the movie *Cheaper by the Dozen*, based on the lives of motion efficiency experts Lillian and Frank Gilbreth, the latter goes so far as to pull out his stopwatch and measure how quickly his brood descends the stairs when summoned. Actual laborers of the 1910s were probably less amused by Gilbreth's use of the stopwatch, which he used to map out the movements of bricklayers, typists, and even baseball players. In fact, another proponent of scientific management, Frederick Winslow Taylor, was brought before a senate subcommittee and questioned about his own understanding of labor, as labor proponents were certain that the efficiency movement was a means to worker exploitation.

There's a great deal of antipathy toward the measurement of social media efforts. In 1999, authors of the book *The Cluetrain*

Manifesto called upon businesses to bring down the barriers of communications between the internal organization and the outside world. While social media has helped to make this clarion call a reality, many organizational leaders are still reluctant to embrace this new openness and transparency. Thus, when social media evangelists like Scott Stratten and Gary Vaynerchuk speak to businesses, they ask their audiences to look beyond return on investment (ROI), arguing that not all value is measurable.

How each organization approaches the use of social media metrics will differ. At every conference I attend on conversion optimization, I hear that we must adhere to the concept that social activities should clearly align with sales. Some organizations have larger strategic frameworks that increase the complexity of how they measure social. The Coca-Cola Company's recent presentation on its Liquid and Linked initiative is one of the most inspiring and enlightened social media presentations I've seen. The animation, narrated by Jonathan Mildenhall, lays out a strategy that covers different types of storytelling across different media, supported by social media. Obviously, for such a campaign, the metrics are going to span many different data points and won't have a direct correlation to the sale of any particular bottle of carbonated beverage.

Processes lend themselves to measurement.

—Joe Dager

The exigencies and realities change dramatically at different scales of business. How a small or microbusiness can use social media, and what it should be measuring, is going to be different from what a large organization can accomplish and must measure. Big is different.

In my own company, we have created a tremendous amount of value through our online social activities. The fact that ours is an online marketing company that provides social media marketing might render it a poor example—but still, I think the circumstances are worth consideration.

The first difficult thing to measure is the amount of effort we've put into social. For one, I personally have put countless hours into social. But then all entrepreneurs tend to put a lot of hours into their business. Second, there is a blurry line between my doing social media for my own pleasure and doing it for the business. Larger businesses have this blurriness too; after all, are you doing social for customer care, brand management, or some other aspect of organizational maintenance that doesn't fall directly under marketing? If you have a team dedicated to social media, keeping track of the hours isn't that difficult, whereas if you have a portion of your executive team doing social, the line is blurrier.

Back to my own company: we've met new employees online, and they, in turn, have introduced us to new business partners and clients. We've met people who run their own agencies and now bring work to us. Through social media, I met the people who are publishing this book, and other people who have invited me to speak at their conferences. A new business development director has come on board—someone I met through a Twitter group—who has in turn brought in a large amount of business based on his own social media connections. Of course, each single business is so different: we could be talking about a professional services company, a consumer packaged goods manufacturer, or any number of other business types. You need to consider your own value chain.

WHY WE MEASURE

We measure for two primary reasons:

1. To inform our efforts so that we can adjust. This is Boyd's OODA Loop in action.
2. To help business decision makers make decisions—to keep them informed of the efficacy of our efforts—to *justify*!

It's tempting to base our measurement needs on the wonderful charts and reports that existing social media monitoring and website analytics provide, but this is backward. Instead, we should identify what we need to know and then work with the tools to try to gain that intelligence.

For instance, if we're doing an influencer project, we'll really want to keep track of when an influencer mentions our brand. Right now, we have to manually keep track of that information, as no tool provides it. There are ways to create custom queries, but a person still needs to go in and pull the actual piece.

This approach is quite different from large data-set analysis, where the tools represent the only way to acquire the right information. For instance, if I'm working with a large national brand, and I'm concerned with overall sentiment, it is not feasible to sample much data manually.

Aligning with Organization Strategy

The *value chain* was introduced as a concept by Michael Porter in his 1985 book, *Competitive Advantage*. His model of the value chain shows the major segments of a business organization with the support infrastructure layer. The main segments are inbound logistics, operations, outbound logistics, marketing and sales, and service. In a *Harvard Business Review* article six years later, Porter describes how the Internet has provided additional value at each of the links in the chain as well as each of the several support layers. A marketer could take that same model and layer on social media, identifying each place where social can provide value. In this way, by tying social in with larger organization strategy, you can identify meaningful metrics.

> If you treat your marketing as a process, then you should be able to measure your marketing.
>
> —Joe Dager

Brainstorm the different ways you can look at the people for whom you can create value and in turn can create value for your organization—that is, who can join you in the market? At DragonSearch we have customers, potential customers, and influencers of both of those groups. You may choose to add a dimension of different customers' lifetime value (LTV), and view your landscape in those terms.

Another model that I mentioned in Chapter 4, on desired outcomes, was the Balanced Scorecard model developed by Drs. Robert Kaplan and David Norton. The Balanced Scorecard uses four perspectives in providing a strategic framework for a company: financial, internal business processes, learning and growth, and customer. I might be using a particular vendor simply because I've been using him and I don't have a convenient alternative. From a financial perspective, that vendor might be satisfied with its profits; however, if that company doesn't also make investments into those other areas of the scorecard, as soon as I have an alternative, I'll be bailing on that vendor, and its profits will plummet before it is able to remedy the situation. I can easily imagine this scenario in the context of a particular cell phone service company that many customers have used simply because it was, for a while, the only alternative with a particular desired smartphone.

Much business thinking is traditionally based on a company-centric mode of thought. Lately, there has been a great deal of discussion about turning that thinking on its head, developing a customer-centric model. One model that has emerged is that of *co-creation*, in which organizations don't simply create things, bring them to market, and make a sale. In the co-creation model, organizations and their customers create value together. The DART model of C. K. Prahalad and Venkat Ramaswamy proposed that value is created through dialogue, access, risk-benefits, and transparency. When considered in light of social media, this model not only can be an integral part of an organization's renewal and success but also seems to be predicated on the very notion of social media. In a 2009 article, Venkat Ramaswamy wrote that management and organizations "must move beyond activities and processes, to interactions as the locus of value creation; beyond the competence base of the firm and its suppliers, to networks of firms and communities of individuals as the source of competence; beyond product and service offerings to meaningful experience environments as the basis of value to individuals; and beyond business processes, to co-creative engagement platforms as the means of creating advantage."[1]

It's not my intention here to discuss every major strategic business philosophy of the past few decades but to point out that there are different ways to conceive of business metrics. It's likely that the leadership outside of marketing would be driving those strategies, but if not, there is an opportunity for marketing to help lead the way beyond a narrow focus on lagging measures like profits.

Net Promoter Score

Frederick F. Reichheld was at a conference where he heard Andy Taylor, the CEO of Enterprise Rent-A-Car, talk about how the company had reduced its client feedback questionnaires to just a couple of questions. Taking the notion even further, Reichheld, along with his client companies, did some intensive research and came up with what they determined was the one question companies should be asking their customers: "On a scale of 1 to 10, how likely is it that you would recommend our brand to a friend or colleague?"

People who answer 0 to 6 are considered detractors, while people who answer 9 or 10 are considered promoters. Those in between are simply considered neutral. The net promoter score (NPS) is arrived at by subtracting the percentage of detractors from the percentage of promoters.

There is an elegant simplicity to the NPS in its focus on revealing your enthusiastic customers. Reichheld's research showed that the NPS was an accurate predicator of a business's health. While a lot of people have taken issue with the validity of Reichheld's findings, the popularity of NPS has taken off since Reichheld wrote his 2003 *Harvard Business Review* article.

If your organization has adopted NPS, you might find ways to allow social media to play a part in boosting the score.

> **Takeaway:** Leaders of marketing teams may not be dictating the larger organizational strategy, but they should be aware of it in developing the appropriate metrics for social media. If the larger strategy doesn't exist, marketers can help bring to leadership an awareness that social media can help drive more significant strategies than focusing on profit alone.

Mapping Social Metrics to Business Metrics

As I discussed in earlier chapters, a series of goals and objectives are feasible in social media. They range from actual sales to very fuzzy concepts such as likeability. And then, on the other side of the aisle in the world of business objectives, you might have objectives like growing the business 20 percent, increasing revenues this year by 10 percent, increasing brand equity, increasing brand awareness, and so on. It's as though we've taken the world of *Star Wars* and are seeking to map it to the world of *Star Trek*. There are distinctive overlaps, but, for the most part, these are two different worlds.

Mapping social metrics to business metrics is necessary to better communicate to stakeholders how social media fits into the overall business ecosystem. If someone is asking why $1,000 should be invested in social media conversations instead of in an advertisement, or instead of being distributed to shareholders, you need to have a cogent explanation. Making an argument for the value of social isn't so simple. When Jonathan Mildenhall of Coca-Cola gave his Liquid and Linked presentation at Cannes, he explained the company's objective of doubling sales by the year 2020. From there, he laid out how conversations, storytelling, and social media are to play a role.

Aligning with Organizational Goals

It is important to clarify goals. We often hear from business leaders such things as "Our big goal is to increase sales by 20 percent." But they seldom mean just that. They might mean, for instance, that they want us to increase sales by 20 percent while maintaining our leadership in our brand's niche. And depending on other market factors, that might mean that we want a larger share of the existing market—or that we wish to grow the market. Sometimes, as marketers, it is our job to help get those goals clarified so that we can integrate them into marketing efforts.

Whatever goals are ultimately identified, you'll want to create a funnel leading from these goals to specific strategies. For instance:

Goal: 10 percent increase month over month sales of blue platinum widgets by end of 2013, while maintaining perception of being trendy.

Strategy: Whenever people speak of blue platinum widgets, or the problem that blue platinum widgets solve, we want our brand name to be associated with that conversation 25 percent of the time, as opposed to 4 percent currently.

Social Metrics Challenges

There are a number of measurement challenges in social media marketing. First, it often isn't feasible to expect measurable results immediately. For instance, if we're placing emphasis on influencers, all we can measure immediately is our activities. We're acting in the absence of a feedback loop.

On the other hand, if our key performance indicator (KPI) has more to do with quantity—having a high volume of connections, for instance—we could start to measure that immediately.

Another measurement challenge involves instances where media and data are disconnected, such as when someone connects via Twitter, then calls on the phone. A similar scenario occurs when someone visits a website, then calls. The software used in analyzing such traffic can determine with a certain degree of reliability that that call resulted from a click on the website, but not with 100 percent certainty. In this way, we connect a flow of leaps across media, from the social ecosystem to the business ecosystem, with a degree of uncertainty. Each organization, each marketer, has different thresholds of tolerance for this uncertainty.

WHAT WE MEASURE

We measure three main groups of actions in social media:

1. **Relationship.** These are measures of when people agree to somehow create a relationship with us. Some of these behaviors are passive, such as signing up for our e-mail list or bookmarking our site's website. Both indicate a willingness to receive communications from us or to revisit our site. Relationship actions can be private (I'm bookmarking this page) or public (I like this page).
2. **Amplification.** These are behaviors where the user somehow amplifies our communications. The communication may be interpreted, remixed, mashed up, or simply shared. We have passed that person's curatorial muster. Amplification actions include retweeting, sharing, e-mailing to a friend, and reposting.
3. **Dialogue.** In some form or another, we are communicating with one another. These communications may be singular and one-way, or a back-and-forth. Sometimes these actions are overt, as when a person comments. They can also be more subtle, such as when a person responds to any piece of communication on the page (for example, ranking a piece of content). The communication might be subtle, but it nevertheless constitutes dialogue.

There are several dimensions to the measurements:

Quantitative—how many? These measures tend to be the simplest and come naturally from computers. We need to create tools to find the measures that matter, not base our measures on the tools available.

Qualitative. This is where measurement becomes difficult. How do you measure the quality of a hug or a kiss? How do you measure the wonderfulness of a dinner party? Just because something is difficult to measure doesn't mean we shouldn't try. If we can move from 100 percent uncertainty to 50 percent uncertainty, that's progress. Refinement will come with time.

Influence. All social media activities have differing levels of influence on other people. A simple "like" will have an infinitesimally small influence on others. One hundred thousand such likes might have a considerably greater influence on other site visitors. A mundane comment on your blog from Salman Rushdie might create quite a stir, while an extensive and thought-provoking comment from the guy down the street might not.

Scalability. We're also faced with the challenge of making measurements in a scalable fashion. If your site receives thousands of comments every day, it might not be feasible to do anything more than sampling.

Velocity. Another aspect of measurement is velocity. If people are engaging with us or amplifying our content, how quickly are they doing so? Velocity offers another lens on reality. On one hand, we can measure how many new followers we've attracted in the past month; on the other, we can measure how long it takes us to grow by a given percentage. Velocity was a key component in John Boyd's thinking around military tactics. In order to succeed, you need to be more agile and swifter than your opponent is. How quick is our own response time? How quickly are we able to design and implement new creative social campaigns?

MEASURES OF INFLUENCE

Each marketing manager must take a measure of her industry and determine the scale in which she is working. If you're selling a major megabrand consumer good, your approach to influencers is going to be quite different than if your company manufactures the motors that go into wheelchairs. With a megabrand, you would need to depend on automated measures of influence. With a niche product, you might want to track your world of influencers in a spreadsheet and assign your own values to each one's level of influence.

- ▶ Connections
- ▶ Level of Influence
- ▶ Share of voice
- ▶ Reach
- ▶ Measuring influencer impact

Quantity of Connections

Many social media marketers will tell you that the number of friends you have on Facebook, followers on Twitter, or people in your circles in Google Plus doesn't matter. But you know better. You know, for instance, that not only is the CEO watching those numbers, but so are the other individuals who see your pages. The quantity of friends, followers, or fans doesn't really mean you're going to better engagement, but it does represent a *social proof*—and when others see that you have a credible quantity of connections, they will be more apt to want to connect as well.

Another outcome of having a higher volume of connections—and I'm not talking about being connected with nonpersons or closed accounts—is that even if the connections are not of the highest quality, the volume provides you with the ability to be agile in later work.

Level of Influence

In an influencer campaign, the idea is to get a certain number of influencers to engage with or talk about our brand. If we focus on engagement, the talking-about should follow. Setting out to measure engagement with a small set of influencers is a very different matter from seeking to increase the overall engagement you might have with your customer base in general.

Let's say that in our social media project, we're setting out to connect with five key influencers. So far so good—we can most certainly determine who those individuals are. We want those influencers to engage with our brand. We could say that different actions represent different levels of engagement. For instance,

- ▶ If influencer retweets something we posted. (OK, that's nice.)
- ▶ If influencer comments on our blog (Now we're talking!)
- ▶ If influencer blogs *about* our blog (Bingo!)

You can go through your own list of actions that matter to your organization, and even give them a score. Some other actions of note:

▶ Referring a friend
▶ E-mail
▶ Tweet
▶ "Like" on Facebook
▶ Print page
▶ Download white paper
▶ Subscribe to e-mail

TABLE 10.1 Rating Engagement and Influence of Key Influencer Actions

	LOW INFLUENCE	HIGH INFLUENCE
Low Engagement		
High Engagement		Sweet Spot

We could say that there are levels of engagement—A, B, C—and that we want a certain quantity of engagements at each level. You can use a chart similar to Table 10.1 to rate levels of engagement and influence of various key influencer actions.

Another problem is that there is an element of quality at play. For instance, a very influential person may comment on my blog with something like, "Hey, great blog post. I totally agree with that idea about blue widgets." The next day, another influencer comes onto the blog and leaves a thoughtful 250-word comment. Of course, the latter is going to have a lot more value. The same is true for even a microblog post: Senator Smith might tweet something like, "nice to see Acme Corp doing its thing in Boston" versus "hey @AcmeCorp, what you're doing in Boston is a real value to the whole community."

So now there are three factors we care about:

1. Quality of engagement
2. Level of influencer
3. Level of engagement

Each of the factors is subjective and requires a person to make a value judgment. Someday it might be possible for computers to determine the quality of an engagement, but at this time, they are still struggling with the automated measurement of sentiment in 140-character microblog posts.

In reference to websites, analytics expert Avinash Kaushik believes that engagement is not really a metric that's well understood or that drives action and improvement on websites. "Engagement is not a metric that anyone understands and even when used it rarely drives the action/improvement on the website." But in this case we're talking about the realm within social media, not just a website.

The means for measuring engagement are bound to be imperfect, but the important thing is that we have a tendency to measure toward a truth. As Henri Matisse said, "Exactitude is not truth." Marketers need to pay attention to engagement, strive to improve engagement, and possess a means to set benchmarks and measure improvement *so that the team can improve.*

Share of Voice

In conventional advertising, *share of voice* indicates the percentage of your brand's advertising within the market. For instance, if there were 1,000 minutes of advertising on national television for paper towels, how many of those minutes were dedicated to my brand of paper towels? In social media marketing, the concept becomes extended to refer to mentions by individuals. Thus, if there were 10,000 mentions of paper towels (or paper towel brands), what percentage referenced my brand? Share of voice, in itself, is not necessarily a predicator of success in the market. For instance, during an oil spill, the oil company behind the accident might have an extremely high share of voice. As a marketing metric, though, it's generally a good benchmark.

Reach

Reach is actually about *potential reach,* that is, how many people *could* be exposed to your messages. In print, for example, we often talk about the fact that a given publication is sent to, say, 10,000 households, and that each household has, on average, three people, thus the reach is 30,000 individuals. In some cases, publishers even include commercial distribution, such as doctors' offices, to show an even higher potential reach. Reach is one of the most misused numbers, as it is often given without the context. For instance, in discussing reach in Twitter, reach might include the followers of anyone who has retweeted a tweet.

Measuring Influencer Impact

In 2010, The International Association for the Measurement and Evaluation of Communication published a set of guidelines at its Second Annual Summit for Measurement, called the *Barcelona Declaration of Measurement Principles*. The second principal was that "Measuring the Effect on Outcomes Is Preferred to Measuring Output."

The daunting challenge is that in many projects it takes time to get meaningful data. Consider this scenario: you've embarked on an influencer project wherein the objective is to get 10 main influencers talking about your brand or participating in your community. There will be a period of time when the team will be engaged in a lot of activities but when it wouldn't yet be reasonable to expect results.

At times like this, it is necessary to measure the activities themselves. This is the best you can do, but at least you can predict a certain likelihood of results based on experience.

You could gather these various activities into one activity report to watch trends and outcomes. For instance, you could maintain a running spreadsheet like Table 10.2. Over time, you'll be able to make reasonable predictions about outcomes. The real outcomes depend on so many variables that there must be a range of predictability. For instance, the quality of your blog comments on influencers' blogs will have a large impact on whether those comments stimulate conversation.

TABLE 10.2 Social Media Activity Report

ACTIVITY TYPE	DATE	QUANTITY
Facebook friend	6 Oct 2012	25
Twitter likes	6 Oct 2012	46
Twitter direct @'s	6 Oct 2012	12
Blog comments	6 Oct 2012	5

MEASURING OUTCOMES: THE GREAT ROI DISCUSSION

Whether social media marketing provides ROI for businesses is one of the hottest topics of debate within the online marketing community. To date, at least two books have been published

with *social media* and *ROI* in the titles, hundreds of articles and
blog posts have been written, and many, many heated debates
have transpired in the halls of conferences like Conversion Conf,
Search Marketing Expo, and Blog World Expo.

Would you want to know the ROI of your mother?

—**Gary Vaynerchuk**

There are those who simply hold that this is a moot discussion—that in order to have value, social media doesn't need to
demonstrate ROI. On the other hand, there are those who frequently have to have that discussion with the C-suite and know
that a plausible answer is needed.

Every time I hear "social media ROI," a unicorn dies; a kitten dies.

—**Scott Stratten**

Often, management wants a clear set of numbers that demonstrate return on investment. If the organization's website includes
e-commerce, it's easy to show that traffic from social sources has
driven a certain part of the sales. The challenge comes into play
when we start talking about last-click attribution, or cases where
there isn't a clear line between social media and the actual sale.

Last-Click Attribution

Last-click attribution refers to the practice of giving credit for an
online conversion to the last source that brought the user to the
website. It would be wonderful if we could know that a person saw
a billboard, then an ad on a train, then searched Google for our
brand, heard about the brand a few times from friends, and then
came to the site and made a purchase. But acquiring that level of
knowledge isn't feasible. In high-volume consumer goods, we can
see changes in sales in a test area—say, after those billboards have
gone up—but it's very easy for the data to get mixed up with other
variables.

Still, in other verticals, the typical time frame from awareness
to purchase might be several months or even over a year. How do
we reconcile these challenges with the C-suite's need to pull the
right levers to manage the organization? When the boss wants to
know why you're putting $100,000 into a social media endeavor

instead of just adding it to the paid search portfolio, will you have the answers?

If your organization needs more sales over the next six months, social media *may not* be the answer. Or, if you have e-commerce and you can create a brilliant campaign, it *might* be feasible.

Alignment with the Customer Funnel

One approach to the ROI discussion is to align social media outcomes with the customer funnel. As mentioned before, the customer funnel was first devised as a tool for salespeople to better understand that customers exist in different phases in relationship to the company. The old funnel, known by the acronym AIDA, was *awareness, interest, desire, action.* Later, the funnel was extended to include *satisfaction* (or advocacy). The old AIDA funnel has been the target of a lot of criticism by people who argue that the paths customers take are a lot more complex. While this argument is valid, the basic funnel is still a valuable tool in understanding the big-picture view of our customers' relationship to the company or products.

> What's the ROI of putting on your pants in the morning?
>
> **—Scott Monty,** the head of social media for Ford

Social media tends to have a strong effect on the two extreme ends of the funnel: awareness and advocacy. It certainly *can* have an influence on interest and desire, and it probably has the least influence on action. Action is where the consumer pulls out the credit card and makes the purchase.

The business should own the data indicating overall market size and the portion of that market that is aware of your brand. While such studies can be costly, it is also possible to understand the relative size of interest (the customer is aware of your brand, and has a positive opinion of it), desire (of those with a positive opinion, who is likely to purchase in a time period), and action (of those who are thinking of making a purchase, what percentage actually does).

☑ CHECKLIST

- ☐ In a team meeting, document the measurements you'd most like to make, regardless of whether such measurements are possible using the tools at your disposal.
- ☐ Document what you are currently measuring
- ☐ Document what you could measure (the capabilities of the tools at hand).
- ☐ Brainstorm ways to measure more of what you would like to measure, and discuss with technicians or programmers to determine if there are viable ways to do so.

CHAPTER 11

EGG ON YOUR FACE
AVOIDING THE BIG MISTAKES

──── GAFFES, FAUX PAS, SCREW-UPS . . . ────

Imagine a revolution taking place in a country where millions of people take to the streets, hundreds are killed, even more injured, and as a result, the nation's leadership resigns. Then an American clothing designer puts out a message saying, "Millions in uproar—rumor is they heard our new spring collection is available online." Venerable clothing designer Kenneth Cole tweeted that message in February and March 2011, kicking off a season of the biggest gaffes in corporate social media since the inception of Twitter.

Less than two weeks later, Gloria Huang, a social media specialist at American Red Cross, got her HootSuite accounts mixed up and tweeted, "Ryan found two more 4 bottle packs of Dogfish Head's Midas Touch beer . . . when we drink we do it right #gettingslizzerd."

On March 9, someone tweeting on behalf of Chrysler Motors posted, "I find it ironic that Detroit is known as the #motorcity and yet no one here knows how to f**king drive." Before the week was out, not only had that individual lost his job, but the marketing agency responsible for Chrysler's Twitter account was dismissed.[1]

In April, a 36-year-old radio ad salesman from Hugo, Minnesota, received a call from the CEO of Aflac offering him a job as the voice of the duck used in Aflac advertising. Dan McKeague had beat out over 12,500 other aspiring quackers for a job left vacant by the firing of comedian Gilbert Gottfried after Gottfried made unfortunate jokes in the aftermath of the tsunami that struck Japan.

Gaffe, faux pas, fumble, stumble, screw-up, goof-up, snafu: whatever you call them, unplanned and unanticipated mistakes will always be a part of marketing. Considering the nature of social media and the nature of people, there's a pretty high likelihood that any organization will eventually put something out on social media that it will regret. Minimizing the likelihood of such communication mistakes and handling them with tact are key skills for marketers working in social media.

Some organizations respond to mistakes by trying to create more controls on social media communications, which has the unfortunate effect of causing those communications to simply be less effective. It is, after all, the very nature of social media to be quick and responsive. If you accept the importance of social media, you must prepare! Short of having each and every piece of communication vetted by your public relations *and* legal teams, the only way to completely prevent such gaffes from occurring in your organization is not to use social media. Some companies in highly regulated industries like food and pharmaceuticals *do* practice such vetting. Imagine two large columns on a whiteboard: "Potential Risks of a Big Screwup" and "Benefits of Social Media." The risks can be pretty bad, but they are not likely to outweigh the potential benefits if some basic procedures guide your use of social media.

Social media success stories make for less interesting news and thus are usually not as well known. When community manager Brandie McCallum couldn't find anyone to help her check in at the JetBlue counter, she tweeted something to that effect. Within minutes, a representative from JetBlue tweeted back with the news that she was contacting the office at the airport and help would be on the way—which in fact it was. Brandie was only too happy to share her love of JetBlue with her thousands of followers, but the incident didn't get the same sort of attention a major goof-up would have.

Some mistakes we make as individuals, and some we make as organizations. Some mistakes seem innocent enough, like the schoolteacher who posted to her Facebook wall a photo of herself drinking a glass of wine while on a European vacation—and then found herself fired from her position at a public school in Georgia. Sometimes, mistakes are more egregious. People older than 30 didn't grow up with social media. Millennials, by and large, have a good sense of what to show and what not to show, but earlier generations can be somewhat flummoxed by the notion of private/private versus public/private versus public/public.

MONDAY MORNING QUARTERBACKING

If we study all of the gaffes and fumbles that have been featured in the news and in the blogosphere, we can discern some pretty clear patterns. I titled this section "Monday Morning Quarterbacking" because it's easier to spot the gaffes in retrospect.

Technology and Software Issues

In both the Chrysler and the Red Cross events, the primary cause of the mistake was that people on the social media team were using tools for both the organization accounts and their personal social media accounts. People who work in social media tend to be active users of social media in their personal lives, which is often part of what makes them effective social marketers. It's imperative that the tools used at work not be the same as the tools used for personal social media. If the team uses one tool for the company accounts, team members should use a different tool for their personal accounts. Doing so would have prevented a great deal of anguish for Chrysler and the Red Cross—not to mention the ad agency and the employee who lost jobs in the Chrysler incident.

On some social media channels, people have personal accounts as well as professional accounts they're responsible for. It is easy for someone to be logged into one account and think that he's logged into another. Unfortunately, this is the way some platforms, such as Facebook, have been developed: organizations are discouraged from having accounts that aren't based on actual people.

As better enterprise-level social media tools become more common, this type of gaffe will probably become history. In many industries, those types of tools will become *de rigueur* if for no other reason than for legal compliance, as organizations will be required to make records of all of their communications no matter what medium is used.

Issues with Education and Training

One of the great hopes of social media is that, eventually, the idea of a separate social media team will simply disappear, just as did the ideas of having a separate team for answering phone calls and e-mails. Eventually, social media will be ubiquitous across all of an organization's departments. At Kenneth Cole, a company long associated with charitable causes, the boss himself was in the front line of communication. A good PR veteran would say that even (and perhaps especially) executives need ongoing communications training. Cole himself has said, "And I filter myself now. But I still love that I have this viral platform to talk to people."[2]

In early 2010, a Vodafone employee posted some offensive comments on his corporate UK Twitter account. While Vodafone was quick to apologize and dismiss the errant employee, this type of event points to the need for more thorough social media training.

Social media professionals are fond of saying that sometimes it's not a social media problem but an HR problem. It's true that the organization would have an issue if an employee publicly made racist or sexist remarks in any public forum; it's just that social media allows such types of public communication to happen so much more easily.

We can't assume that every new hire is in full possession of social media common sense. But at least we can decrease the likelihood of these types of mistakes with thorough training.

If you think that controlling all of the social media tools with work-flow management will prevent a mishap, consider the two Domino's employees who created a video of themselves engaging in unsanitary pranks in a Domino's kitchen. They posted their video directly to YouTube. Is this an HR problem or a training problem?

Values Misalignment

In analyzing hundreds of social media gaffes, I've found that many involve misaligned values—either organizational values out of alignment with customer values, or organizational values not being upheld. When Go Daddy CEO Bob Parsons made a video about killing an elephant, it created a media furor. Some people have argued (as is often the case with media mishaps) that the backlash was actually a net positive for the company, while others maintain that there was a serious erosion of the brand's equity.

In 2010, Walmart made its Facebook page more fashion oriented, a move some observers felt didn't reflect the company's core value proposition. Walmart also precluded users from sharing information on a discussion board. The move made the company look bad, as some users felt Walmart was trying to control the conversation.

Nontransparent or Disingenuous Responses

In October 2011, ChapStick released an ad on its Facebook page picturing a woman bent over a couch with her backside facing the camera. The caption, "Where do lost ChapSticks go?" and the image filename, ass.jpg, were offensive to some people, who posted complaints on ChapStick's wall. ChapStick, in turn, started deleting the comments. The fact that the brand wouldn't engage in discussion and even went so far as to silence its customers only served to further infuriate the public.

In the early days of social media, people often assumed different identities, but as the media matured, an ethos of transparency and authenticity emerged. In this environment, if you make a mistake, it's important that you own it and be open and frank about it. After Netflix made some astonishing missteps in a proposed restructuring of its services, Reed Hastings, the CEO and cofounder of Netflix, authored an apologetic blog post that has so far garnered close to 28,000 comments, over 58,000 Facebook likes, and 5,000 tweets. Sometimes publicly owning a mistake is painful, but it allows the brand to move forward.

What is the value of transparency? If people feel that you are being open and frank, you are more apt to earn their trust. And as we saw in Chapter 8, trust is a major factor in influence.

Reacting and Not Reacting

Organizations often react strongly to their social media bases in a way that backfires. In one case, a tenant of an apartment building complained on Twitter that her building's management company was insensitive to the presence of mold. The management company responded by suing the tenant for $50,000 in damages. Had the company not sued, the tenant's complaint probably would have gone no further than her 15 followers. But the lawsuit created a tremendous amount of media coverage. The case was mentioned in a *Huffington Post* blog about how people need to be careful about what they tweet, the suit was dismissed by the court, and the management company is forever branded as heavy-handed.

Large companies can make this mistake as well. Nestlé asked its fans not to use an altered version of the company's logo in their profiles. It further antagonized its fans by making strong statements about intellectual property. Along those same lines, many large companies have shut down nonofficial Facebook fan pages created by customers. Coca-Cola, by contrast, actually encouraged such a page. To this day, it's one of the most successful Facebook fan pages in existence. In social, everything you say or do is on the public stage. We often tell individuals that they should never post anything in social media that they wouldn't want their mothers to read. Companies should never post anything they wouldn't want on the front page of the morning news.

You must be careful that your social media policy in itself doesn't cause you to overreact. When Dallas Cowboys cheerleader Melissa Kellerman was accidentally tackled by a player, she wrote a cute tweet, "Not hurtin' today, like some of y'all thought I would be! Our TE [tight end] isn't as tough as he looks . . . That or I'm WAY tougher than I look. ;)" It's unclear whether the Cowboys subsequently forced Kellerman to delete her Twitter account or if she did so willingly, but, as CNET blogger Daniel Terdiman wrote, the "Cowboys look tone-deaf and vindictive."[3]

Not reacting can be every bit as problematic as overreacting. If you have good social media monitoring and procedures in place, you need to respond to gaffes. Your customers will perceive absolute silence or a delayed response as the absence of caring. And if you don't care, you're not going to have influence.

The Snowball Effect

Often, social media gaffes have multiple parts. BP's response to the *Deepwater Horizon* oil spill in the Gulf of Mexico is a case in point: a narrative of the disaster reveals a series of gaffes that didn't end until long after the well was plugged.

Kenneth Cole was extremely quick to retract his tweet, but when apologetic signs were in place at stores the very next day, there were rumors that the whole thing was preplanned. In all likelihood, KC did a rush job at the printers, but the takeaway is this: in your moment of penance, don't be too polished; allow yourself to be seen as human and imperfect.

ChapStick's original gaffe was its off-color advertisement. Humor has a way of doing that. But the company's really big mistake was deleting the posts on its Facebook wall. Once the genie is out of the bottle, don't even think of trying to put it back in, as that will almost certainly create an even bigger problem. And make sure your social media team knows this as well, because a well-meaning employee can delete a post and the move can blow up in your face.

RECOVERY

The good news is that organizations can take several steps to reduce the likelihood of social media gaffes.

First, take care in handling customer communications and consider the underlying implications of what you communicate. Zappos decided to correct the spelling and grammar of its customers' reviews, based on research showing that consumers are more likely to trust sites with well-written content. In doing so, the company compromised the authenticity of the reviews. Also, in correcting customers' grammar and spelling, it was as though Zappos were holding up a sign that said, "You're broken and need fixing." Not a great way to establish a social connection.

A Botched Recovery

On September 27, 2011, the marketing team for Ragú spaghetti sauce sent a tweet to "daddy bloggers" asking, "Do your kids like it when you make dinner?" The tweet included a link to a video in which three "mommy bloggers" suggest that dads take cooking dinner less seriously than mothers do. One blogger who received the tweet was author and marketer C. C. Chapman, not only a strong voice in the social media marketing community, but an ardent proponent of issues important to fathers.

Chapman wrote a blog post entitled "Ragú Hates Dads," criticizing Ragú for the video and for spamming him with the tweet. Chapman shared his thoughts with 29,000 followers on Twitter. Ragú initially responded with silence. Finally, after several days, Ragú reached out to Chapman with a phone call and responded to some comments on *another* blog—from an account picturing a jar of spaghetti sauce as its avatar.

As with the Kenneth Cole event, Ragú followed one mistake with another, like a pileup on a Los Angeles freeway. The first mistake was the video itself. Using irony can be dangerous territory for any brand to play in (though, as the Old Spice campaign demonstrates, irony can also be successful). The next mistake was spamming daddy bloggers. The third mistake was Ragú's initial failure to respond to Chapman. The fourth mistake was Ragú's unconvincing public response to Chapman, which didn't even come from an individual but from "Ragú."

Recovering Gracefully

Often, the biggest problem isn't the mistake itself but the follow-up. In the examples mentioned in this chapter, Aflac did a great follow-up job by being extremely quick in firing Gottfried, which, given the gravity of the circumstances, was probably the best response.

That same response by Chrysler, though, might have been a bit heavy-handed. At the end of the day, Chrysler actually got some negative feedback for making too strong a response. It was important for Chrysler to show its loyalty to Detroit, but when Chrysler (or, for that matter, anyone) tweets, it's read across the world. One possible alternative response would have been to announce that the company was providing the person who wrote the tweet with some lessons in anger management—then to insist that the whole thing be documented on social media as well. Chrysler could have had some fun with it. Also, it turns out the agency was fired not for making the mistake but for not being truthful about it. Chrysler missed an opportunity to be open about the incident and create goodwill.

That's exactly what happened with the Red Cross tweet. Certainly, no potential or existing donor to Red Cross wants to learn that the Red Cross team is off on a bender. Perhaps because of their extensive experience working within crisis moments, Wendy Harman, social media director at the Red Cross, immediately replied, "We've deleted the rogue tweet but rest assured the Red Cross is sober and we've confiscated the keys."

Impressed by the tweet's bonhomie (which could easily have been more like the Chrysler response), fans of the Dogfish Head brewery started using the hashtag #gettingslizzerd, calling for people to donate money and blood to the Red Cross.

Many people have suggested that the Kenneth Cole tweet was designed to create an uproar and that Cole was prepared for the backlash. He might have been subscribing to the sentiment of P. T. Barnum, who liked to say, "There's no such thing as bad press, as long as they spell your name right." On the other hand, a quick Internet search brings up dozens of branding pundits who assert that real damage has been done to the brand.

Remember, a key element of influence is likability. So whatever response to a social media faux pas you might consider, think about whether it would be the response of a likable person.

1. Consider your community. Doing the microsegmentation work and developing a good understanding of your community will help you communicate appropriately.
2. If a mistake has been made, apologize. If an action has been misconstrued as a mistake, apologize for the impact. You can also ask the community what else you could do to rectify the mistake. Ekaterina Walter of Intel said, "Be prepared to tell your customers that the people running your page are human beings, and you need to just come out and say, 'we all make mistakes.'"
3. Monitor your social media and if your organization can afford to do so, make that monitoring and response capability available over weekends and holidays as well.
4. Apologies should come from a real person. It isn't easy to feel that a jar of sauce is penitent.
5. Be timely. Many social media crises could be averted with more timely responses. By letting people remain angry, you increase the chance that a small issue will become large. Timeliness relies on monitoring. If you're not constantly monitoring, you're not going to be a quick responder.

Of course, you must consider the source and scale of customer unhappiness. Is the person lodging the complaint a troll, that is, someone who does nothing but complain on social media and will never be gratified by any response? If so, it might be best to avoid engagement. Is the person (or his spouse) a social media maven? Or anyone with a community? You'd better follow up, and take that follow-up seriously.

PREVENTING MISTAKES

The basic elements of mistake prevention are policy, procedures, training, and really great people. Initial training should be provided to all team members, describing the types of communications that are inappropriate, how to handle criticism online, and what steps should be taken in the event of a mishap.

It's also important to have a general policy and to ensure that the social media team is fully acquainted with it. This is more than a social media policy for the entire company, however. This policy should address possible social media missteps.

At DragonSearch, we frequently discuss fumbles that occur at other companies and issues that could have become fumbles by our own team. For instance, during Hurricane Irene, one of our team members posted a fairly innocent remark about how people had fared in the storm, but he paired the remark with an image of a product. In light of the Kenneth Cole gaffe, our team felt that we should avoid even the slightest appearance of trying to capitalize on an event where lives and property have been lost. We now have a policy that we never reference a disaster in our communications in social media except to express concern for everyone's well-being.

For most clients, we also avoid any discussion of religion or politics, unless religion or politics are part of a company's core beliefs. For instance, most of our clients are supportive of gay marriage and are willing to communicate that in social media. Some, however, prefer to be circumspect so as not to offend customers who don't share the company's view.

Top Five Responses Document

Stephanie Weingart of BlueGlass Interactive recommends that social media teams create a document comprising the five most frequently needed responses. With time, you can expand this document to include the top 20 or 30 responses. Each member of the team should be familiar with the document and have easy access to it when needed. As Marcy Massura pointed out, it's convenient if this top responses document is also vetted with legal or other departments. In this way, even in an organization that requires that responses go through an approval process, many common responses can be preapproved and thus posted more quickly.

The Crisis Project

The crisis project details a company's plans in the event of a major crisis (be it related to social media or otherwise) such as a personal injury, oil spill, high-profile legal problem, and so forth. First, it's good to be aware of the types of crises your organization might face. BP certainly was aware of the possibility of a major oil spill. A manufacturer should know if someone could be injured by its products. If you look at the history of your industry, what sorts of crises have occurred?

In the event that your organization is responsible for an injury—to an employee, customer, or anyone else—you should be prepared to make a thoughtful response. You may be scared to make any statement, but if you don't make one, your organization will appear cold and uncaring. If you have a public relations department, coordinate your emergency response plan with the PR people.

✔ CHECKLIST

Top Considerations for Avoiding Social Media Mistakes

- [ ] Avoid mixing the technologies used for the organization's social media with individuals' personal accounts.
- [ ] Ensure that employees both on and off the social media team receive training.
- [ ] Think before deleting or editing users' comments or posts. Could it cause a backlash?
- [ ] Respond quickly.
- [ ] When a mistake is made, sincerely apologize.
- [ ] When appropriate, use humor.
- [ ] Have a policy in place.
- [ ] Have a top-responses document prepared to be used.

CHAPTER 12

CREATIVE JUICE

THE LABORATORY FOR INNOVATIVE SOCIAL MEDIA

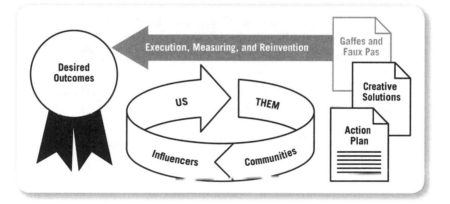

— CREATIVITY IN ACTION —

It wasn't so long ago that in order to shave his face, a man would take out his shaving brush and work up some lather on a bar of shaving soap in a cup before applying it to his face. In the early 1920s, Clinton Odell worked with a chemist to create a cream that didn't require all that brushing; the result was Burma-Shave. One of Odell's sons, Allan, finished up a stint at college and joined the business as an itinerant salesman, trying to get stores to stock the new product on spec. During his travels, the younger Odell noticed roadside signs for gas stations that were spaced apart, advertising gas on one, groceries on another, and perhaps food on yet a third. Driving along, he'd find himself anticipating the next sign, and he thought Burma-Shave could make use of this device.

Back at the home office, the son went to his father with the idea. Clinton Odell finally agreed to contribute $200 to test the idea. Allan and his brother Leonard created some signs and posted them along a Minnesota highway. Each sign had a word or phrase that continued on subsequent signs, leading to a final sign that read "Burma-Shave." For example:

Are your whiskers
When you wake
Tougher than
A two-bit steak?
Try
Burma-Shave

The signs were a huge success, and orders for Burma-Shave skyrocketed. Eventually, Burma-Shave erected more than 7,000 sets of signs across the country. At one point, the Odells felt that their ideas were drying up, so they created an annual contest inviting people to submit their own rhymes. The winners were awarded $100 each. The contests received an average of over 50,000 submissions each year.

Imagine your delight driving the highways, seeing the first sign, the second, and so on until you got to the punch line. Depression-era consumers thought it was pretty nifty, resulting in over $3 million of annual revenue (up from $60,000 annually during the previous decade). The signs became an icon of American roadsides.

The signs' effectiveness later diminished when people started driving a lot faster on America's highways, and the Burma-Shave brand languished. Finally, Gillette acquired Burma-Shave and licensed out the brand for some small product lines. The signs were removed and used to repair barns and bridges. A few made their way to museums.

CREATIVITY MUST MEET THE BUSINESS NEEDS

The common perception of advertising and marketing involves brilliant brainstorming and shouts of "Eureka!" This sensibility persists into the age of social media marketing—the idea that in order to be successful with marketing campaigns, you need to have brilliant creative. Like the Burma-Shave campaign, there are countless examples of wonderful marketing efforts that garner attention, awards, and even increased business; those are the campaigns the executive suite points to, saying, "That's what *we* need!"

Hollywood has done its share to perpetuate the notion of creativity-driven marketing, with TV shows like *Bewitched* and *Madmen*, movies like *Cohen's Advertising Scheme* (1904 from the Edison Studio), *How to Succeed in Business Without Really Trying*, and dozens of other films that portray advertising and marketing executives experiencing great "Aha!" moments. For marketers, the equivalent of winning the lottery is coming up with a novel idea that sparks the delight of the masses, bringing throngs of new customers through the door.

Many marketing agencies go into initial client meetings with a portfolio of imaginative ideas; in turn, many brand executives have grown to expect such presentations. These presentations, however, usurp the smart marketing process, and neither the agency nor the brand benefits. In fact, these presentations can lead decision makers to lock into a concept before the business requirements have been fully developed, resulting in wrong-minded, wasteful campaigns. Instead, creative campaigns need to be constructed on a bedrock of good traditional marketing research.

We all want to create campaigns like Burma-Shave's, those bits of marketing that become part of our cultural heritage, win industry recognition, and dramatically increase revenues as well. Whatever creative ideas you generate, however, the outcomes still need to be in alignment with your organization's culture. Having a thorough understanding of your organizational vision, brand personality, and customer microsegments will guide your efforts. Instead of leading with the brilliant concepts, marketing campaigns can be developed using a series of steps that help the marketer. The major steps are laid out in the overall process discussed in this book:

- ▶ Goals and objectives identification
- ▶ Audience segmentation
- ▶ Audience segment needs
- ▶ Influencers

Marketing campaigns can be successful in one sense but not another, failing to meet the business needs. For years, Aflac was

wildly successful at increasing its name awareness through marketing. At a certain point, though, Aflac realized that it needed to
shift gears so that not only would just about everyone in the U.S.
market know the Aflac name, but they'd also understand what
Aflac *does.*

COMMON ELEMENTS OF SUCCESSFUL SOCIAL MEDIA PROJECTS

One of Gillette's competitors in the modern era is Old Spice, a
brand that was created in 1937 by William Lightfoot Schultz.
Procter & Gamble acquired Old Spice in 1990 and began to
transition the brand image from one of a gray-haired father's
aftershave to a younger person's antiperspirant. By 2004, Old
Spice had garnered the highest market share of men's antiperspi-
rants, but much of the consumer market still regarded the brand
in the context of nostalgia.

P&G brought in Wieden + Kennedy to help remedy the
brand's dated image. Wieden + Kennedy demonstrated the power
of segmenting audiences and identifying influencers. At a pivotal
point in the Old Spice campaign, they identified media influencers and created videos that actually responded to those individuals
by name.[1]

But even that campaign went through a series of developments,
originating with the television ads and then progressing to the
online videos and social media responses. Creative directors Jason
Bagley and Eric Baldwin credit much of the magic to actor Isaiah
Mustafa's on-the-spot humor. A lot of people were involved in a
series of online interactions that developed over a small period of
time: in that first series of online video responses, the team shot
87 short videos in 11 hours.

The big splash project (BSP) is the type of social media project
that is most likely to generate news coverage and spark discussions
at marketing conferences. That now famous Old Spice campaign
was a BSP, as was the "My Starbucks Idea" program, Burger
King's Sacrifice, and the BMW 1 Series Graffiti Contest. There is
nothing intrinsically wrong with the BSP, especially if the project
helps to build community or get the attention of influencers.

In reviewing hundreds of campaigns, I have observed certain
common elements among the most successful. (And by success, I

mean campaigns that garnered a great deal of media buzz. Whether or not they actually generated revenue is another matter, and is typically a well-protected bit of information.) The elements are

1. Fun
2. Unexpected
3. Participatory
4. Cross media
5. Storytelling

Fun

A preponderance of successful campaigns are just plain fun. Every so often, an inspirational campaign takes off and spreads like crazy, but by and large, fun wins the day. Almost all of the major social media campaigns that have gone wildly viral have had a strong component of fun. When the CEO of Blendtec puts an iPhone into a blender, we're all 12 years old again, murmuring "cool" under our breath. Many of the websites associated with these campaigns allow users to participate in a lighthearted way, such as the OfficeMax Elf Yourself or the CareerBuilder Monk-e-mail sites that allow you to insert your own image into an animation. All of these campaigns can trace their heritage back to those Burma-Shave signs, where fun lifted spirits and attracted customers. Sex might be thought of as another great way to catch attention, but when it comes to the majority of viral social media, fun dominates. (Figure 12.1 lists more aspects of videos that are likely to trigger sharing activity.)

Unexpected

Activities that offer small unexpected payoffs are addictive. The unexpected tickles the brain and gives it a microshot of dopamine. This is why novelty is so critical, and why copying a previously successful concept often fails.

Almost every car company is now sponsoring road trips to be videotaped and shared, and countless companies are trying to replicate the success of the Pepsi Refresh campaign. While these efforts might have some success, they just aren't going to have the same impact as the original. Novelty is about the unexpected.

Customer care folk wisdom holds that customers don't like the unexpected. That's true when it comes to a service that doesn't

12 Video Triggers
An aspect of the video likely to trigger sharing activity

BODY

FUNNY . . . ROFL!

Humor is notoriously subjective: will your audience be tickled by a witty quip or a banana slip? Parody or farce? Either way, a top-notch "pay-off" is a must-have.

HOT . . . sexy!

This one is a slippery pole, ranging from booty-shaking through celebrity upskirts and full-blown sex tapes. Approach with caution: this is hot stuff: misjudge your target audience and you'll get your fingers burned.

SHOCKING . . . OMG!

As a species we find disturbing content strangely compelling. There's a certain thrill in being frightened by the unexpected and the ghastly; hence, the popularity of car-crash TV and hard-hitting road safety ads.

UNBELIEVABLE . . . AWSM!

Has to be seen to be believed. Brilliantly done stop-motion sequences, people performing on the edge of what's humanly possible, creative teams pushing the boundaries of human and technological achievement.

CONTROVERSIAL . . . GENIUS!/F**** S***

Love it or hate it? Some videos divide opinion and split the online community into opposing and vociferous factions. Not for the faint of heart. You'll need to be prepared to stand your ground.

MIND

GLEEKY . . . COOL!

This is brain-food for aficionados. Could be the unboxing of a limited edition game for Xbox fans, a Jen Aniston meta-viral for meme fiends, or Sue Sylvester voguing for *Glee* fans.

ILLUMINATING . . . FIRST!

Will open your mind and rock your head. Unveilings, sneak peeks, breaking news. Eye-opening facts, trends, or technology. Useful as well as entertaining. Guaranteed to make your synapses tingle, or your money back.

RANDOM . . . WTF?

Confounded, surprised? Bewildered? Random clips often involve a verbal, visual, or conceptual non sequitur that is as funny as it is bewildering. Why is that gorilla playing the drums? I Like Turtles? You bet we do!

ZEITGEIST

Does this video ride the crest of a current meme or develop a current news story? Does it capture the public mood or celebrate a public holiday? Timing is everything. Yesterday is nothing.

SOUL

CUTE . . . AWWW!

Sneezing pandas, laughing babies, fainting kitties, these are the videos that melt our hearts.

UPLIFTING . . . YAY! I love this!

Want to escape the tedium of everyday life? Bring a smile to the faces of fed-up friends? For a shot of Feel Good factor 40, look no further. Flash mobs, group dances, and good causes tend to coalesce around this trigger.

MOVING . . . WOW. Made me cry.

These videos are intense, with the power to evoke strong emotions: hope, pride, faith, nostalgia, love, anticipation. The best ones give us goose bumps, uplift our souls, and renew our faith in humanity.

FIGURE 12.1 Twelve video-sharing triggers *(Copyright © UNRULY Media 2011, reprinted by permission)*

work, a package that doesn't arrive, or a medical procedure that causes more pain than anticipated. But when it comes to niceties, the unexpected is best. In one study of restaurants that gave unexpected small gifts to customers as they entered the business, sales increased by 40 percent. When the same gifts were expected by the customers, the increase in sales did not occur.

Participatory

A hallmark of social media is the notion of participation: others can be a part of the story. Allowing people to participate has been a key element of dozens of top social media campaigns.

In the Night Agency's Hoodie campaign for Champion, consumers were invited to create their own hoodie designs. A winning design, chosen through online voting, was ultimately made into an actual piece of clothing.

When you enable the outside world to participate in your brand, you have to be willing to relinquish a certain amount of control. For instance, if you invite people to make their own videos and upload them, you may not always like what you get. The results might be out of line with your brand.

In order to help your campaign be more participatory, go through each step of the campaign and ask yourself where consumers could be allowed to participate. Can the audience be allowed to finish an element or be asked to contribute one of their own? Can they vote? Can they get access to special information by participating?

The Pepsi Refresh campaign is a great example: people were asked to submit the names of nonprofit entities that could benefit from a cash grant. The winning entities were chosen in an online vote. Advocates for different entities rallied on their behalf, getting even more people to get involved.

In Target's Bullseye Gives program, users are asked to vote on how Target will give away 5 percent of its income. As users vote on the Facebook page, they are also able to publish their votes back to their own feeds. So while both Pepsi and Target are aligning their brands with caring about people, they are doing so in a way that allows their customers to participate and encourages them to help spread the brand name.

The Pepsi and Target campaigns are examples of brands cocreating value. Instead of simply giving away millions of dollars, a brand can work with its customers to give that money to causes. As a result, the consumer will have a stronger association with the brand.

Cross Media

In 1997, Blendtec's marketing director George Wright used an inexpensive video camera to capture the company's CEO testing blenders on various objects. The videos resulted in millions of views and a substantial gain in the company's sales. That sort of runaway success is still possible online, but it's not as easy as it was during the early days of YouTube. Many of the most popular social campaigns today have the advantage of mainstream media first. The Old Spice videos, Burger King's Subservient Chicken, and Evian's Roller Babies all appeared in television commercials, which provided an enormous boost to the spread of the videos online.

Unruly Media is an agency that helps videos spread through social media more quickly. In the case of Evian's Roller Babies,[2] which has had over 45 million views, the agency extensively researched influencers and posted teaser videos two weeks before the official launch.

Large media buys are just one way to work across media. In *The Dentsu Way*, a book about the famous Japanese advertising agency, the authors talk about intentionally creating an information gap that induces word-of-mouth communications. For example, a website might suggest part of a story. Subway signs might then suggest more of the story, encouraging users to share the story on their cell phones or on social media. In this way, the user becomes a part of the story.

Dentsu's approach might more properly be referred to as "transmedia storytelling," as opposed to simply cross media. A key element of transmedia storytelling is the continuation (not simply the reiteration) of the narrative in different media. In other words, unique aspects of the story are embodied in each medium. Henry Jenkins is a professor at the University of Southern California, where he frequently speaks and writes on transmedia storytelling. He suggests several core principles of transmedia storytelling that are worth exploring by marketers:[3]

1. Spreadability vs. drillability
2. Continuity vs. multiplicity
3. Immersion vs. extractability
4. Worldbuilding
5. Seriality
6. Subjectivity
7. Performance

In a very natural way, marketers have been posting content on their blogs, sharing with their social networks, and then using those very same social networks to bring audience members back to the blog. People post both photos and videos to their favorite networks, which then draws people over to their pages on other platforms. Social media is not only integral to transmedia storytelling, but transmedia storytelling is intrinsic to most social media.

Marketers are leaving a lot of value on the cutting-room floor when they don't take advantage of this aspect of social. Gary Vaynerchuk pointed out that even the successful Old Spice campaign missed out on a lot of value when the company didn't follow through to create enduring connections. Vaynerchuk wrote in his book *The Thank You Economy*, "Old Spice saw a major spike in sales and brand awareness, but there are plenty of brands that have done great marketing, spiked for a while, and then disappeared off the consumer radar. The brand had an opportunity to continue the conversation with all of those people who connected with them, and they squandered it. The left their customers behind, limiting the full impact the campaign could have had on the brand."

With any campaign, be prepared for success. What if the results exceed your wildest dreams? Be prepared with ways to keep you new connections engaged with you. How could Old Spice have kept Gary Vaynerchuk happy?

Storytelling

Storytelling is embedded in our psyches. The prehistoric cave paintings were probably used to help in telling stories, just as similar rock paintings are used by aboriginals today. Storytelling is found in every culture around the world. In advertising, even the best print ads tell stories, not only with copy but with images. It is natural that we bring storytelling into our social media efforts as well.

In a recent presentation, representatives of Coca-Cola talked about dynamic storytelling with "incremental elements of a brand idea that get dispersed systematically across multiple channels of conversation for the purposes of creating a unified and coordinated brand experience." They went on to identify five key facets of storytelling:

1. Serial storytelling
2. Multifaceted storytelling
3. Spreadable storytelling
4. Immersion and discovery storytelling
5. Engagement through storytelling

Coca-Cola has taken the concept of happiness and used it as an underlying theme in all of its communications. When the global insurance company Aflac focuses its Facebook wall posts on helping children with cancer, the company is telling stories—stories of the children themselves, stories of the doctors fighting the disease, and the overarching story of how Aflac is a caring part of the larger community.

Nancy Duarte, in her wonderful book about giving presentations, *Resonate*, suggests that in being an effective storyteller, we don't play the role of hero but instead allow our listeners to play that role. A question worth asking on a regular basis is, "How we can help our customers or audience be the hero?"

When bringing storytelling into social media marketing, consider the classic elements of storytelling: beginning, middle, climax, ending, and character development. Plan out a calendar or timeline in which you introduce certain elements. If you have a particular event scheduled in the future, you could build the story toward that event as a climax.

Saatchi & Saatchi Copenhagen created a video for clothing company Quiksilver showing a group of kids who throw a stick of dynamite into a city pond and then surf on the resulting wave. The video was viewed over 35 million times worldwide and resulted in a 10 to 20 percent sales increase.

One aspect of the Quiksilver campaign is that it created information that was of interest to surfing publications, which published stories about the video. The content was very much in alignment with the values of the company's customers—irreverence to cultural norms and rules, and finding fun in unorthodox albeit dangerous ways. Likewise, the Old Spice campaign was built on a reexamination of who the customer was. Most advertising for men's body products was geared toward the male buyers themselves, but research showed that girlfriends and wives were often the ones who purchased the products. Knowing your audience is still a basic marketing premise that holds true in digital marketing every bit as much as it does in traditional media marketing.

HOW TO CREATE AN INNOVATION HOTHOUSE

Social media teams often get too caught up in the day-to-day activities of brand management. They nurture connections, have conversations, and help bring influencers into the communities that surround the brand—so much so that they sometimes forget to consider the creative and innovative uses of social media that outside agencies often bring to larger clients. The problem is that too often large creative campaigns fail to bring new audiences and connections into deeper engagement with ongoing social activities.

Know When to Bring Creative In

In order to bring the wildly creative type of social media into the brand, you must make time in the daily and weekly busyness for the creative spark to ignite. The time must be built into the process. There are at least two major opportunities for creative brainstorming:

1. When the project plan is being developed. Right then and there, make sure that time is allocated for creative thought.
2. When objectives aren't being met. "We were supposed to have 10,000 Facebook fans by this week, and we only have 5,000?" Time for a creative meeting.
3. When the organization's goals or objective have shifted.
4. When there are timely opportunities. When Sarah Palin, the Republican running mate to presidential hopeful John McCain, was taken to task for purchasing expensive designer clothes, a blogger for a noted discount outlet made a lot of noise, suggesting Palin should have shopped at the outlet. The mainstream press picked up on that notion, and our client's name was prominent in the news for several weeks.

Use Brainstorming

In 1939, frustrated advertising executive Alex F. Osborn developed the brainstorming method of ideation. Two key aspects of Osborn's method are an "anything goes" mentality and an emphasis on getting the ideas out quickly. Many variations on ideation have been developed, but the basic technique remains the same. The more the team completely understands the larger marketing picture, the more effective ideation is going to be. Take the time to fully familiarize the entire team with the market segments, differentiators, and larger marketing strategies in the brand.

Brainstorming will be more effective if you separate your team from the normal distractions of the office, like e-mail and phones. Ask that all cell phones, smartphones, and tablets be turned off.

Find a meeting place outside of your normal office as a means of changing the way people think. If you are considering bringing in outside creative talent, do so in the brainstorming session with the internal team members; the outside vendor will be brought up to speed more quickly, and the internal team will benefit from the outsiders' view.

Provide a Creative Environment

Whether for a particular meeting, such as a brainstorming session, or for the social media team's work area, consider creating an environment in which people are encouraged to think in innovative ways. Place large pieces of paper or pasteboard on common wall areas where photographs and words can be pasted or taped. Environments like those of large technology companies simply aren't designed to make employees feel like work can be fun, but the world of play is where we often come up with new ways of thinking.

Our daily work reinforces our cognitive patterns, so when it's time for creative thinking, it can be challenging to get out of the rut. Rolls of paper, markers, stickers, scissors, and magazines that can be torn up are excellent items to have on hand. Abstract puzzles (such as building blocks) can bring an element of play to the room and, in turn, help change how people think. Even wearing masks can change the way people think and get the group in a more playful spirit.

When Paul Klee taught art at the Bauhaus, he kept a journal of his teaching ideas, later published as the *Pedagogical Notebooks*. In them, you can see where he has taken ideas from nature, for instance, in diagramming the way water and nutrients flow up through the many roots of a tree, up the trunk, and through the branches and leaves. This is a classic example of how designers and artists work—by seeing the underlying patterns of the world around them, deconstructing them, then reassembling the parts into a cohesive whole.

In creating social media projects, we benefit from getting out of our social media professional heads and playing tricks on ourselves, shaking things up so that we think differently and see those underlying patterns. Bring out the social media pyramid diagrams, and use them to discuss the relative merits and features of different platforms. Place diagrams of the salient social platforms on the wall, and find connections between them so that you can uncover ways of extending stories across different platforms.

Have Ceremonial Beginnings

Kick off creative brainstorming sessions with a formal announcement of ground rules, such as "all ideas have a place" and "make room for your other team members to be heard." Avoid getting fixated on the quality of any particular idea, and move quickly to get a lot of thinking out on the table. Start with a breathing exercise or a game of "What is your spirit animal today?" This can help isolate workshop time from the rest of the day and put everyone at ease by changing the pace.

Brainstorm with People from Other Parts of the Organization

Ekaterina Walter of Intel suggests that in larger organizations, you spur innovation by bringing people from the various parts of the organization into the meeting: "Create something like a think tank, internally, where people can feel free to bring ideas to you that can help you brainstorm. A lot of times we work in silos, so I think it is as simple and as hard as establishing a path for these ideas to escalate and elevate toward those points or those teams who might have influence to secure additional budget to see this idea happening or see it happening on a global scale. I think it's just as easy and as hard as that, and it all has to do with internal culture and internal processes."

Because social media are basically technology-based, the creative solutions might very well have a technical aspect; thus, it's important for creative people to work closely with the technology people. At the Night Agency, Evan Vogel says, "We sit down with the engineers and our developers and of course on the more traditional side, the strategist and the creative directors." Vogel sees it as an advantage to have the technologists in the same room as the people executing the social media plan.

Revisit Audience Subsegments

If your social media efforts are getting stalled, or you're creating a new initiative, return to the microsegment brainstorming that I discussed in Chapter 6. Take a fresh look at the microsegments. What is it about this or that group that hasn't been working?

In one of our projects, we found that one microsegment, the publicists for well-known musicians, was being unresponsive. They would give our client a shout-out in social media, but they were reluctant to commit to repeat messages. Looking at our microsegments, we turned to some of the groups that we hadn't yet interacted with, like luthiers and instrument case makers. While not getting the big impact we might have gotten with, say, a Lady Gaga shout-out, we were able to reenergize the campaign through engagement with those smaller groups.

Also, by putting microsegments brainstorming back up on the wall, the team was able to look at it again with fresh eyes and create some new concepts. Basically, microsegments provide a lens, a different way of looking at the world before us. The communities of those microsegments provide yet another lens. What do people get out of being in those communities? If a given community wanted to change something in the world, what would it be? Knowing that, how might you change how you interact with that community?

Change the Pace

Jazz musicians will often take a piece and go into double time for a few bars, then bring it back to the original tempo. If you feel that the brainstorming is plodding along, do something to change the pace. Ask everyone to write down three new ideas in one minute. Ask them to write down three new ideas that someone else (such as a coworker or a celebrity) would come up with.

Beyond Brainstorming

There comes a point in brainstorming when the flow of new solutions ceases—the team is stuck. At that point, it may be useful to try more structured approaches in creative solution finding. In the 1940s and 1950s, while interned in a Soviet gulag, inventor and science fiction author Genrich Altshuller developed a theory of problem solving for the purpose of more effective invention. His theory was called TRIZ, an acronym for the Russian phrase that translates as "The Theory of Solving Inventive Problems." He and others studied thousands of patents and identified patterns of how problems tend to be solved. Out of that research came an understanding that while the number of problems might seem infinite, there are a set number of solution types.

A related approach, called Unified Structured Inventive Thinking (USIT) was developed in the Ford Motor Company Research Laboratory, and yet another related approach, Systematic Inventive Thinking (SIT), was developed in Israel. People practicing TRIZ, USIT, and SIT have typically spent a fair amount of time in training. What I'm looking for is ways that marketers can adapt these techniques to find creative solutions in social media.

SIT consists of three common phases: problem definition, problem analysis, and application of solution concepts. In the problem definition phase, the problem is stated in terms of objects, attributes, and a single unwanted effect. In many ways, this relates to the Scrum method of storytelling described in Chapter 3.

These innovation techniques share a common feature with Six Sigma—that solutions come out of a thorough and robust analysis of problems. Some of the approaches discussed earlier in the book, such as microsegmentation, are aspects of problem analysis.

When defining a marketing problem for structured innovation, don't think only in terms of the project at hand. For instance, my problem isn't that I want to create buzz on Facebook. The problem is higher up the food chain. My problem is that I want to gain more of the market for a particular product, but the market is constrained, or I'm facing a challenge in differentiation, or potential customers don't discern strong value propositions between opposing products—or whatever the case may be.

In TRIZ, a set of 40 principles were identified, based on solutions to problems—typically in engineering. Over the years, various people have applied those principles to customer relations, sales, and marketing problems. Some of the ideas may not translate quite so easily or might require some poetic interpretation.

Dr. Roni Horowitz extended the thinking of TRIZ, developing what he called ASIT (Advanced Systematic Inventive Thinking). He elaborated on TRIZ by adding the element of the "closed world" condition, which favors the use of existing resources in lieu of introducing new features or elements to a problem solution.[4] He also introduced the notion that instead of resolving contradictions, solutions should achieve qualitative change.

Instead of 40 principles, Horowitz proposed five tools:

1. Unification: assign a new use to something that is already in a system
2. Multiplication: solve a problem by introducing a modified copy of an existing object into the system
3. Division: solve a problem by dividing an object and reorganizing it parts
4. Break symmetry: solve a problem by changing a symmetrical situation into an asymmetrical one.
5. Object removal: solve a problem by removing an object from the system

While Altshuller and Horowitz weren't thinking about problem solving in marketing, their tools for problem solving are useful. Break the problem down into parts. For instance, if we were trying to increase donations to a nonprofit, we might consider:

- ▶ Audience (How does it break down into segments based on various criteria such as demographic, psychographic, microsegments, etc.?)
- ▶ The appeal (What draws various segments of the audience to give to this type of organization?)
- ▶ Audience attitude toward the organization (Is it known? Is it liked?)
- ▶ Impediments to people giving to this particular organization (Is the known audience cash-strapped because of the recession, or do they prefer other organizations, etc.?)
- ▶ The method of giving (Is the giving process difficult logistically? Do most of the people who like this type of organization lack credit cards, or do the places where they give lack the necessary machines?)

✔ CHECKLIST

- ☐ Good creative campaigns tend to have one or more basic elements: fun, unexpected, participatory, cross media, or storytelling.
- ☐ Use brainstorming, build time for creative solutions into projects, and provide a creative environment.
- ☐ Consider using structured brainstorming techniques.

CHAPTER 13

HERE WE GO AGAIN

MEASURING AND IMPROVING THE
SOCIAL MEDIA MARKETING PROCESS

─── INTEGRATED ONLINE MARKETING ───

One of the promises of online marketing is that the various buckets can be integrated, one helping to create more value in another. The three main buckets to consider are social media, paid online media such as pay per click (PPC) and display, and search engine optimization (SEO). A strong presence in all three areas helps to create a greater sense of authority and trust, which in turn strengthens each area as well as your overall brand strength. Of course, the delineation doesn't remain online but influences and is influenced by activities offline such as PR, advertising, and events.

In the integration of online marketing, we know that there is a strong component of research within each area. While the exact nature of the research isn't identical, the findings from each can inform the other. The keyword research done in SEO, in particular, can help inform how we identify microaudiences, communities, and influencers within the social sphere, while the connections we make within social media help build up a portfolio of backlinks that in turn support SEO.

Blogs represent the greatest opportunity to tie in social media with SEO. On the blog, a library of content can be amassed with more and more contextually relevant text. Each blog post is an opportunity to share content with individuals and communities. We've even seen many instances where communities develop around blog posts, with certain people returning time and again to participate in conversations.

Paid online advertising can support social media marketing in a couple of different ways. In paid search results, we can often more quickly identify key phrases that bring converting traffic to our site. That quickness allows us to then focus on those key phrases in both SEO and social media. Conversely, as time-sensitive news or events occur, we can use paid search to drive traffic even to our social profiles or content. Paid advertising on social platforms can also help to support our standing within those communities or to create more influence more quickly, particularly if the advertising is crafted in such a way as not to be overtly promotional.

There has also been a trend in search for social signals to play a stronger role in search results. Google has recently been allowing people to "+1" ads that show up in sponsored results and is showing items in the natural results that have been "+1'd" by people within your social network. Evidence suggests that Google, for one, is looking to more fully integrate the social world with the world of search. By integrating SEO—and by that, I mean SEO that is mindful of semantically contextual content in relation to your subjects—you'll gain more authority and trust in both your social spheres and in search. Figure 13.1 gives an overview of the online marketing landscape.

PROCESS IMPROVEMENT METHODOLOGIES

American manufacturing comprises a story within a story. The ability to manufacture mechanical parts with a certain degree

FIGURE 13.1 Social Media Marketing (SMM) in the online marketing landscape

of precision was first developed in the United States. This technological advance took machinery off the artisan's workbench and meant that parts could be exchanged from one machine to another. If one manufactured item broke, it could be repaired with parts from another. If a device needed a new bolt, it could be ordered from a manufacturer. The methodologies that enabled precision manufacturing, along with a vast wealth of natural resources and a growing population, enabled the fantastic rate of growth of American industries.

At the beginning of the twentieth century, Henry Ford was producing his Model T's on assembly lines. Frederick Winslow Taylor, Frank Gilbreth, and Henry Gantt (developer of the eponymous Gantt chart) applied precision manufacturing philosophies to labor itself, in what would become known as *scientific management*, and laid the groundwork for the *efficiency movement*. As individuals, Taylor, Gilbreth, and Gantt were often at odds with one another, but they shared an interest in the systematic study and recording of motion, tasks, and schedules applied to human labor. Their ideas ushered in the beginning of a U.S. manufacturing hegemony that did not diminish until the 1970s.

At the time of the gas shortages of the late 1970s, the phrase "Made in Japan" did not inspire American shoppers. A generation of poorly made American cars like the Ford Pinto and AMC Gremlin began to erode American's confidence in homegrown products. By the early 1980s, Japanese automobile manufacturers were building plants in the United States, and by 2000, Japan was the leading manufacturer of cars in the world.

Lean

In the 1920s, engineer Walter A. Shewhart developed the *control chart*, a tool used still used in business process and manufacturing for the modeling of statistical controls. Two Americans, W. Edwards Deming and Joseph M. Juran, were heavily influenced by Shewhart's work and, independently of one another, were invited in the early 1950s to lecture in Japan on manufacturing improvement. There was something about Japan—perhaps the postwar condition of the economy combined with ingrained cultural sensibilities about quality—that led the concept of quality improvement to become powerful in Japanese industry. By the 1980s, it was American manufacturers who were inviting Japanese consultants to make improvements to U.S. companies and processes.

Several leaders of Toyota developed what was to become known as the Toyota Production System, a precursor to Lean, which also relied heavily on the thinking of Deming. Lean emphasizes understanding customers and their needs. In eliminating wasteful steps, Lean considers what does not bring value to that customer. Lean also emphasizes acquiring and maintaining knowledge, a critical component to social media teams.

Joe Dager, author of *Lean Marketing House*, provides a six-step process to Lean marketing:

Step 1. Create a value stream map based on your marketing flow.

Step 2. Analyze each process and start asking these questions until you have eliminated all waste from the process:

> Why are we doing this process?
>
> What value/purpose does it serve the customer?
>
> How can we eliminate all waste from this process?
>
> Map new simplified process.

Step 3. Now determine the constraint in your marketing flow:

> Identify the system's constraint.
>
> Exploit the system's constraint.
>
> Subordinate everything else to the above decision.
>
> Elevate the system's constraint.
>
> If a constraint is broken (that is, relieved or improved), go back to Step 1. However, don't allow inertia to become a constraint.

Step 4. Implement and test new process using the Plan, Do, Check, Act cycle.

Step 5. Simplify your marketing flow.

> Eliminate all wasted activities that the customer sees little value in.
>
> Create dashboard with input/output measurements showing daily, weekly, monthly, and yearly progress.

Step 6. Find the value stream ROI and resource allocation.

> Create the future value stream map.
>
> Feedback: develop visual metrics showing progress of the company's Lean continuous improvement program.

Six Sigma

In the 1970s, a Japanese firm assumed control of a Motorola television factory. As a result of its management, defects plunged to one-twentieth of what they had been, and costs actually decreased. In an effort to understand the shortcomings of its manufacturing, Motorola executives and engineers made an intense study of the Japanese firm's success. Out of that work came a philosophy and system dubbed Six Sigma, a name originating in statistical modeling.

While often associated with manufacturing and engineering, Six Sigma has been applied to many other kinds of organizational activity, including marketing. Six Sigma uses DMAIC, which stands for define (goals), measure, analyze, improve, and control. It's easy to see how these steps are closely aligned with the process described in this book, starting with desirable outcomes. Another key element of Six Sigma is that it isn't about quality from an internal viewpoint but about creating quality by improving the customer's value, a theme that is paramount in social media marketing.

Capability Maturity Model

Enterprise software projects are notorious for exceeding both budgets and timelines. Hoping to better control such projects, the U.S. Air Force commissioned a study from Carnegie Mellon University. There, the Capability Maturity Model for Software was developed, defining a set of process areas, practices, and levels of maturity. There are five levels of maturity: initial (ad hoc), repeatable, defined, managed, and optimizing. The model has been extended into other disciplines including human resources, sales, e-Government, and IT related activities.

The Community Roundtable (www.community-roundtable. com) is a peer network of community managers and social media practitioners. Its website was developed as a resource for social media community managers and other people with similar responsibilities. The organization has gathered the thinking of numerous individuals in the industry and created a Community Maturity Model.[1]

The model defines eight competencies and then maps them across four stages of maturity. The competencies are strategy, leadership, culture, community management, content and programming, policies and governance, tools, and metrics and measurement. The four stages are hierarchy, emergent community, community, and network (Figure 13.2).

While the Community Roundtable's model was created from the vantage point of social media as integrated across an organization, it is equally applicable to social media from the marketer's perspective. The original Capability Maturity Models developed at Carnegie Mellon had a very strong focus on documentation. One step we can still take with the community model is to outline the documentation for each area that should be developed and maintained.

─────────── CONCLUSION ───────────

The word *process* can cause people's eyes to glaze over. It conjures up spreadsheets, stopwatches, and possibly a stern-faced

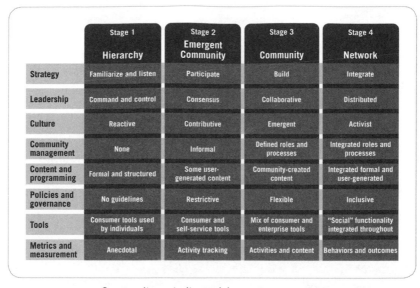

	Stage 1 **Hierarchy**	Stage 2 **Emergent Community**	Stage 3 **Community**	Stage 4 **Network**
Strategy	Familiarize and listen	Participate	Build	Integrate
Leadership	Command and control	Consensus	Collaborative	Distributed
Culture	Reactive	Contributive	Emergent	Activist
Community management	None	Informal	Defined roles and processes	Integrated roles and processes
Content and programming	Formal and structured	Some user-generated content	Community-created content	Integrated formal and user-generated
Policies and governance	No guidelines	Restrictive	Flexible	Inclusive
Tools	Consumer tools used by individuals	Consumer and self-service tools	Mix of consumer and enterprise tools	"Social" functionality integrated throughout
Metrics and measurement	Anecdotal	Activity tracking	Activities and content	Behaviors and outcomes

FIGURE 13.2 Community maturity model *(Courtesy of The Community Roundtable)*

taskmaster. Process, though, is simply the way that we go about doing things. We have a legacy of businesses preceding us that developed process improvement methodologies, and while some of those methodologies may not be applicable, tools are available to help make marketing much more than what it too often is.

The processes and methodologies described in this book are only a beginning of a framework. Almost every statement could have been preceded with a disclaimer of "depending on your industry," or "depending on your organization." You can and must create your own processes and define your playbook.

When I was a child, my father told me to put on my socks before my pants, reasoning that it was just a bit easier. It's possible that a lifetime of putting socks on first won't add up to very much; perhaps, as a process, it wasn't important. But when you have teams of people endeavoring in much more complicated activities, little efficiencies do add up. When less time is spent inefficiently, more value is created. People's lives are spent doing more meaningful work. In whatever business we apply our talents, if we are able to help our organization become more closely engaged with its customers and create more value for them, we've accomplished something special for everyone involved.

NOTES

CHAPTER 1

1 http://www.edelmandigital.com/2011/12/16/social-business-demystified/

CHAPTER 2

1 http://www.northwestern.edu/newscenter/stories/2011/05/twitter-african-americans-hargittai.html.
2 http://socialmediamediasres.wordpress.com/2011/07/09/making-catalysts-the-roots-of-social-media-and-network-building/.
3 http://www.npr.org/blogs/krulwich/2011/02/17/133785829/a-shockingly-short-history-of-hello, accessed August 28, 2011.
4 http://www.sylloge.com/personal/2003_03_01_s.html#91273866, accessed September 2011.
5 http://nform.com/publications/social-software-building-block.

CHAPTER 3

1 "Designing Social Media Policy for Government: Eight Essential Elements," Center for Technology in Government, University at Albany, SUNY, http://www.ctg.albany.edu/publications/guides/social_media _policy/social_media_policy.pdf.
2 http://www.smh.com.au/technology/technology-news/twitter-user-sued -by-exemployer-for-his-followers-20111228-1pbx1.html.

CHAPTER 4

1 See http://www.brewsomegood.ca.
2 David I. Cleland and William Richard King, *Systems, Organizations, Analysis, Management: A Book of Readings*, Institute of Management Sciences, 1960, and McGraw-Hill, 1969.
3 George T. Doran, "There's a S.M.A.R.T. Way to Write Management's Goals and Objectives," *Management Review* 70, no. 11 (November 1981).
4 http://searchenginewatch.com/article/2066784/Be-Stubborn-With-Your -Social-Media-Vision-but-Flexible-With-Your-Plan.

CHAPTER 5

1 http://www.socialmediaexplorer.com/social-media-marketing/finding-your -brand-voice/.

CHAPTER 6

1 http://www.cooper.com/journal/2003/08/the_origin_of_personas.html.
2 http://www.socialconversations.com/2010/03/social-media-case-study -foiled-cupcakes/.

CHAPTER 7

1 http://authenticorganizations.com/harquail/2010/03/31/corporate-logo -tattoos-the-wrong-way-to-wear-the-brand/.

CHAPTER 8

1 Edward Grant, *Planets, Stars, and Orbs: The Medieval Cosmos, 1200–1687.*
2 Gregory S. Berns et al., *Neurobiological Correlates of Social Conformity and Independence During Mental Rotation,* http://www.ccnl.emory.edu/greg/Berns%20Conformity%20final%20printed.pdf, accessed August 25, 2011.
3 Martin A. Nowak, *Super Cooperators,* 241.
4 Marcel Mauss, *The Gift.*
5 *Persuasion, Social Influence, and Compliance Gaining.*
6 Stephanie Gaskell, "BP Will Pay 'Legitimate' Gulf Coast Oil Slick Claims, but CEO Says CO. Not Responsible for Accident." *Daily News,* May 3, 2010.

CHAPTER 9

1 http://mynorthwest.com/?nid=646&sid=520370.

CHAPTER 10

1 C. K. Prahalad, and Venkat Ramaswamy. "Co-Creation Experiences: The Next Practice in Value Creation." *Journal of Interactive Marketing,* vol. 18, no. 3 (2004): 5-14. Web.

CHAPTER 11

1 http://mashable.com/2011/03/09/chrysler-drops-the-f-bomb-on-twitter/.
2 *Harvard Business Review,* December 2011.
3 http://news.cnet.com/8301-13772_3-57331720-52/tackled-cowboys-cheerleader-forced-off-twitter/.

CHAPTER 12

1 http://www.businessweek.com/magazine/content/04_44/b3906116.htm.
2 http://www.unrulymedia.com/case-studies/evian-roller-babies.html.
3 http://henryjenkins.org/2009/12/the_revenge_of_the_origami_uni.html.
4 http://triz40.com/aff_TRIZ_to_ASIT.htm.

CHAPTER 13

1 http://community-roundtable.com/2009/06/the-community-maturity-model/.

REFERENCES

Aaker, Jennifer, and Andy Smith. *The Dragonfly Effect.* San Francisco: Jossey-Bass, 2010.

Albrecht, Karl. *Social Intelligence.* San Francisco: Jossey-Bass, 2006.

Alderson, Wroe. *Marketing Behavior & Executive Action.* Mansfield Centre: Martino Publishing, 2009.

Alexander, Christopher. *A Pattern Language.* New York: Oxford University Press, 1997. Aral, Sinan. "Identifying Social Influence: A Comment on Opinion Leadership and Social Contagion in New Product Diffusion." *Marketing Science, Articles in Advance,* 2010, 1–7. Web.

Azhar, Azeem. "The New Marketing Model: Peer Index Marketing." *Gigaom* 13 (August 2011). Web.

Bakshy, Eytan, Winter A. Mason, Jake M. Hofman, and Duncan J. Watts. "Everyone's an Influencer: Quantifying Influence on Twitter." *4th International Conference on Web Search and Data Mining,* 2011. Web.

Barron, Jennifer, and Jim Hollingshead. "Making Segmentation Work." *Marketing Management,* 2002. Web.

Berns, Gregory S., Jonathan Chappelow, Caroline F. Zink, Giuseppe Pagnoni, Megan E. Martin-Skurski, and Jim Richards. "Neurobiological Correlates of Social Conformity and Independence During Mental Rotation." *Biological Psychiatry* 58 (2005): 245–253. Web.

Blanchard, Olivier. *Social Media ROI.* Indianapolis: Pearson Education, Inc., 2011.

Boyd, Danah "Social Steganography: Learning to Hide in Plain Sight." *DML Central,* 23 August 2010. Web.

Boyd, Drew. "A Structured, Facilitated Team Approach to Innovation." *Organization Development Journal* 25, no. 3 (2007): 119–122. Web.

Brito, Michael. *Smart Business, Social Business.* Indianapolis: Pearson Education, 2012.

Coram, Robert. *Boyd.* New York: Little, Brown and Company, 2002.

Cova, Bernard, Robert V. Kozinets, and Avi Shankar. *Consumer Tribes.* Amsterdam: Butterworth-Heinemann, 2007.

Dunbar, Robin. *Grooming, Gossip, and the Evolution of Language.* Cambridge: Harvard University Press, 1998.

Fine, Gary Alan, and Lisa-Jo van den Scott. "Wispy Communities: Transient Gathering and Imagined Micro-Communities." *American Behavioral Scientist* 55, no. 10 (2011): 1319–1335. Web.

Gahran, Amy. "How to Gain Influence on Twitter? Focus." *CNN Tech.* 7, April 2011. Web.

Gass, Robert H., and John S. Seiter. *Persuasion, Social Influence, and Compliance Gaining.* Boston: Pearson Education, 2007.

Goncalves, Bruno, Nicola Perra, and Alessandro Vespignani. "Validation for Dunbar's Number in Twitter Conversations." 2011. Web.

Gossieaux, Francois, and Ed Moran. *The Hyper-Social Organization.* New York: McGraw-Hill, 2010.

Granovetter, Mark S. *Getting a Job.* Cambridge: Harvard University Press, 1974.

Hagel III, John, John Seely Brown, and Lang Davison. *The Power of Pull.* New York: Basic Books, 2010.

Hanna, Richard, Andrew Rohm, and Victoria L. Crittenden. "We're All Connected: The Power of the Social Media Ecosystem." *Business Horizons* 54 (2011): 265–273. Web.

Haven, Brian. "Marketing's New Key Metric: Engagement." August 8, 2007. Web.

Höök, Kristina, David Benyon, and Alan J. Munro. *Designing Information Spaces: The Social Navigation Approach.* London: Springer-Verlag, 2003.

"How Does NetBase Achieve the Best Accuracy for Understanding Consumers Online?" *Netbase.* September 2010. Web.

Java, Akshay, Tim Finin, Xiaodan Song, and Belle Tseng. "Why We Twitter: Understanding Microblogging Usage and Communities." *Joint 9th WEBKDD and 1st SNA-KDD Workshop* (2007): 56–65. Web.

Jenkins, Henry. "Transmedia Storytelling 101." *HenryJenkins.org.* March 22, 2007. Web.

Katz, Elihu, and Paul F. Lazarsfeld. *Personal Influence.* New Brunswick: Transaction Publishers, 2006.

Kietzmann, Jan H., Kristopher Hermkens, Ian P. McCarthy, and Bruno S. Silvestre. "Social Media? Get Serious! Understanding the Functional Building Blocks of Social Media." *Business Horizons* 54 (2011): 241–251. Web.

Kozinets, Robert V. "E-Tribalized Marketing? The Strategic Implications of Virtual Communities of Consumption." *European Management Journal* 17, no. 3 (1999): 252–264. Web.

Kozinets, Robert V. *Netnography.* Los Angeles: SAGE Publications Inc., 2010.

Kozinets, Robert V. "The Field Behind the Screen: Using Netnography for Marketing Research in Online Communities." *Journal of Marketing Research* 39 (2002): 61–72. Web.

Lannon, Judie, and Merry Baskin. *A Master Class in Brand Planning.* Chichester: John Wiley & Sons, Inc., 2007.

Levine, Rick, Christopher Locke, Doc Searls, and David Weinberger. *The Cluetrain Manifesto.* New York: Basic Books, 2009.

Levy, Sidney J. "Symbols for Sale." *Harvard Business Review* 37 (1959): 117–124. Web.

Lewis, E. St. Elmo. *Getting the Most out of Business.* New York: The Ronald Press Company, 1916.

Linden, David J. *The Compass of Pleasure.* New York: Viking Penguin, 2011.

Lovett, John. *Social Media Metrics Secrets.* Indianapolis: Wiley Publishing, Inc., 2011.

Marchand, Roland. *Advertising the American Dream.* Berkeley: University of California Press, 1985.

Marchand, Roland. *Creating the Corporate Soul.* Berkeley: University of California Press, 1998.

Mauss, Marcel. *The Gift.* New York: W. W. Norton & Company, August 2000.

Moxnes, Paul. "Deep Roles: Twelve Primordial Roles of Mind and Organization," *Human Relations* 52, no. 11 (1999): 1427-1444.

Naaman, Mor, Jeffrey Boase, and Chih-Hui Lai. "Is it Really About Me? Message Content in Social Awareness Streams." *Computer Supported Cooperative Work* (2010). Web.

Neisser, Drew. "Hey, Facebook, It's Time for the LOVE Button." *MediaPost*, February 8, 2011. Web.

Nisbet, Matthew C., and John E. Kotcher. "A Two-Step Flow of Influence?" *Science Communication* 30, no. 3 (2009): 328–354. Web.

Nowak, Andrzej, Jacek Szamrej, and Bibb Latane. "From Private Attitude to Public Opinion: A Dynamic Theory of Social Impact." *Psychological Review* 97, no. 3 (1990): 362–376. Web.

Nowak, Martin A. *Super Cooperators*. New York: Free Press, 2011.

Nowak, Martin A., Corina E. Tarnita, and Tibor Antal. "Evolutionary Dynamics in Structured Populations." *Philosophical Transactions of the Royal Society* 365 (2010): 19–30. Web.

Owyang, Jeremiah. "Enhancing Net Promoter Score (NPS) with Total Social Customer Value (TSCV)." *Web Strategy*, 20 June 2010. Web.

Petty, Richard E., and John T. Cacioppo. "The Elaboration Likelihood Model of Persuasion." *Advances in Experimental Social Psychology* 19 (1986): 123–162. Web.

Pincus-Roth, Zachary. " 'Transmedia': A Brave New World In Entertainment Marketing." *Los Angeles Times*, November 22, 2009. Web.

Porter, Michael E. "Strategy and the Internet." *Harvard Business Review*, 2001. Web.

Prahalad, C. K., and Venkat Ramaswamy. "Co-Creation Experiences: The Next Practice in Value Creation." *Journal of Interactive Marketing* 18, no. 3 (2004): 5–14. Web.

Putnam, Robert D. *Bowling Alone*. New York: Simon & Schuster Paperbacks, 2000.

Pyzdek, Thomas. *The Six Sigma Handbook*. New York: McGraw-Hill (2003).

Qualman, Erik. *Socialnomics*. Hoboken: John Wiley & Sons, Inc., 2009.

Raclaw, Joshua. "Two Patterns for Conversational Closings in Instant Message Discourse." *Colorado Research in Linguistics* 21 (2008). Web.

Ramaswamy, Venkat. "Are You Ready for the Co-Creation Movement?" *IESE Insight* (2009): 29–35. Web.

Regan, Dennis T. "Effects of a Flavor and Liking on Compliance." *Journal of Experimental Social Psychology* 7, no. 6 (1971): 627–639. Web.

Richards, Chet. *Certain to Win*. Xlibris Corporation, 2004.

Rittel, Horst W. J., and Melvin M. Webber. "Dilemmas in a General Theory of Planning." *Policy Sciences* 4 (1973): 155–169. Web.

Rosen, Jay. "The People Formerly Known as the Audience." *Pressthink*, June 27, 2006. Web.

Roughead, Adm. Gary. Institute for Public Relations Strategic Communications Summit, 6 June 2011. Lecture.

Shapiro, Benson P., and Thomas V. Bonoma. "How to Segment Industrial Markets." *Harvard Business Review*, 1984. Web.

Shirky, Clay. *Here Comes Everybody*. New York: Penguin Group, 2008.

Smith, Nick, and Robert Wollan. *The Social Media Management Handbook*. Hoboken: John Wiley & Sons, Inc., 2011.

Solis, Brian. *Engage!* Hoboken: John Wiley & Sons, Inc., 2010.

Solis, Brian. *The End of Business as Usual*. Hoboken: John Wiley & Sons, Inc., 2012.

Sponder, Marshall. *Social Media Analytics*. New York: McGraw-Hill, 2012.

"State of Community Management 2011." *The Community Roundtable*, 2011. Web.

Stern, Jim. *Social Media Metrics*. Hoboken: John Wiley & Sons, Inc., 2010.

Stratten, Scott. *Unmarketing*. Hoboken: John Wiley & Sons, Inc., 2010.

Strauss, Liz. "Influence: Do You Know the Value of a Single Dissenting Voice?" *Successful Blog*, August 15, 2011. Web.

Sugiyama, Kotaro, and Tim Andree. *The Dentsu Way*. New York: McGraw-Hill, 2011.

Suh, Bongwon, Lichan Hong, Peter Pirolli, and Ed H. Chi. "Want to Be Retweeted? Large Scale Analytics on Factors Impacting Retweet in Twitter Network." *2010 IEEE Second International Conference on SocialCom*, 2010, 177–184. Web.

Takeuchi, Hirotaka, and Ikujiro Nonaka. "The New New Product Development Game." *Harvard Business Review*, 1986. Web.

Vaynerchuk, Gary. *The Thank You Economy*. New York: HarperCollins Publishers, 2011.

Vickers, Sir Geoffrey. *The Art of Judgment*. New York: Basic Books, Inc., 1965.

Walton, Douglas, and Fabrizio Macagno. "Types of Dialogue, Dialectical Relevance, and Textual Congruity." *Anthropology and Philosophy* 8 (2007): 101–121. Web.

Womack, James P., and Daniel T. Jones. *Lean Thinking*. London: Simon & Schuster, Inc., 2003.

INDEX

ABOUT THE AUTHOR

As a veteran of the digital agency world, Ric Dragon has provided strategic analysis, information architecture, and process improvement for clients including NASA, the United Nations, American Cancer Society, and the Museum of Natural History. He is currently the CEO and co-founder of DragonSearch, where he leads a team of professionals delivering digital advertising, search engine optimization, and social media services to national and international clients. Dragon is a recognized speaker at industry conferences including Blog World, SMX, BrandsConf, and Socialize Conf. Dragon is also a frequent contributor to publications including Marketing Land and Social Media Monthly. He splits his time between the mid Hudson Valley and Manhattan.